Eating *to* Glorify **GOD**

Tamera Shearon

WESTBOW
P R E S S®
A DIVISION OF THOMAS NELSON
& ZONDERVAN

This book is a work of non-fiction. Unless otherwise noted, the author and the publisher make no explicit guarantees as to the accuracy of the information contained in this book and in some cases, names of people and places have been altered to protect their privacy.

All scripture, unless otherwise indicated, is taken from the New King James Version®. Copyright © 1982 by Thomas Nelson. Used by permission. All rights reserved.

Scripture quotations marked (NIV) are taken from the Holy Bible, New International Version®, NIV®. Copyright © 1973, 1978, 1984, 2011 by Biblica, Inc.™ Used by permission of Zondervan. All rights reserved worldwide. www. zondervan.com The "NIV" and "New International Version" are trademarks registered in the United States Patent and Trademark Office by Biblica, Inc.™

WestBow Press books may be ordered through booksellers or by contacting:

WestBow Press
A Division of Thomas Nelson & Zondervan
1663 Liberty Drive
Bloomington, IN 47403
www.westbowpress.com
1 (866) 928-1240

Because of the dynamic nature of the Internet, any web addresses or links contained in this book may have changed since publication and may no longer be valid. The views expressed in this work are solely those of the author and do not necessarily reflect the views of the publisher, and the publisher hereby disclaims any responsibility for them.

Any people depicted in stock imagery provided by Getty Images are models, and such images are being used for illustrative purposes only. Certain stock imagery © Getty Images.

ISBN: 978-1-9736-4635-8 (sc)
ISBN: 978-1-9736-4634-1 (hc)
ISBN: 978-1-9736-4636-5 (e)

Library of Congress Control Number: 2018913809

Print information available on the last page.

WestBow Press rev. date: 11/29/2018

Kirban Reference Bible, King James Version, AMG International, Inc., D/B/A AMG Publishers, 1979.

Women of Faith Devotional Bible, New King James Version, Thomas Nelson, Inc., 2003.

This book is dedicated to:
my children and their husbands—
Jessica and Noah, Aubrey and Wesley, Leila and Christopher;
my granddaughter, Chloe;
my mother and father, and my sister and brother

A special dedication goes to Pastor Dave Divine who ...
inspired me to move out from under the pomegranate tree
(First book of Samuel, chapter 14)

Faith is an Act

In memory of
Johann Sebastian Bach
March 31 (O.S. 21 March), 1685–July 28, 1750
"JJ and SDG"

Therefore whether you eat, or drink, or whatever you do, do all to the glory of God.

—1 Corinthians 10:31

A special thank-you to. …

Jesus, for all Your help

To God alone I give the glory

Contents

Introduction

I T WAS A BEAUTIFUL afternoon as I headed to visit with a friend of mine. While driving, for no particular reason, I moved my hand over my throat, only to discover that my lymph nodes were sore. I really thought nothing of it. But, as the day continued into the evening, I noticed that my lymph nodes were getting even sorer. Within six hours of my initial discovery, the slight tenderness turned into a very painful condition. Lying down added to the discomfort. By the next morning, I had so much swelling that, at times, swallowing was difficult. By three in the afternoon, I found myself in the emergency room. Just the slightest touch of my shirt collar rubbing against my neck sent me into agony. Tears came to my eyes when the doctor had no choice but to touch them during his examination. I was sent home with antibiotics and painkillers. The diagnosis was acute lymphadenitis. By six o'clock, I was home, waiting for the painkillers to kick in and trying to find some relief. By the time the painkillers started to take effect, six more hours of agony had transpired, and I had taken twice the prescribed dosage. It was nearly midnight by that point, and my children had arrived to tend to my needs. Later that morning, I couldn't even swallow. Even using a straw to take in fluids was unbearable. I saw my primary physician, who gave me an injection of antibiotics and referred me to an ear, nose, and throat (ENT) specialist.

I sat in the ENT's exam room, nearly in tears from the pain, and received the worst news I could have been given (or so I thought at the time). The doctor feared I had lupus. There was no other possible, or even probable, reason from my condition. Nothing else could explain it. My world and life just stopped. It was one week before Thanksgiving, and I was three-quarters away from finishing my training for the marathon I was going to run in Las Vegas for Crohn's disease—an event I was not going to be able to participate in. Eating was too difficult, and I did not think that I would be well enough, or even somewhat better by then. My training for Rock 'N' Roll Las Vegas was over; my running had come to a sudden halt.

There I was, a forty-five-year-old who should be in her prime, and yet I was faced with these medical problems. This latest diagnosis of lupus was only an addition to the other problems I'd had in the six years prior. This is not the prequel of my history; it begins much further back than this. To complete this story, I must start at the very beginning, so you can understand what I have endured and suffered, finding very little help from doctors. But, through my own discoveries and research, I found my way back to health in a whole new and from a whole new perspective. But is it *really* new? What I discovered is not exactly what the doctor ordered, but it is *exactly* what God intended.

Heavenly Father, give me the ability to tell my story so that others will not have to suffer as I have. Provide me the words that I may write to inspire others to have health, prosperity, and true happiness in living and eating healthy. May they listen to Your words and commit to Your will, with all of their hearts, bodies and souls. Lord, I ask you to bless the ones who hold this book in their hands, and I pray that through this book they find Your love and blessings, just as I have. Amen.

Chapter 1

The Rest of the Story

September 4, 1996, was my first day at the fire-department training center for Firefighter 101 Recruit School. That was when I found a love for running. I ran a lot in the navy, but that was because I had to rather than wanted to. Being healthy and having endurance, I discovered, was a huge necessity for the job of fighting fires. I weighed only 105 pounds and stood just 5' 3" tall, and this left many people to doubt that I would even complete the class, much less pass. But, as with most recruit classes, you first become a team and then a family. They encouraged me just as much as I encouraged them. Sometimes I even felt my brothers had more confidence in me than I did. I wondered sometimes if my strength was derived from not disappointing them, rather than for seeking my own success. I made it, and on graduation day, my class gave me a standing ovation as they heard my name called and I walked to the front to receive my certificate of completion.

The next thing I remember—just as any other firefighter can and will recall—is my first day at my first station assignment. Station 2,

Sandy Springs, Georgia, the busiest station in the county. As I recall, the guys bragged all the time about being ranked right up there with New York City firefighters when it came to running calls. There was a waiting list of other firefighters wanting to be at that station. It was the dream of dreams to be at Station 2 and wear that same patch that so many others had worn before me: the embroidered patch with a firefighter holding a baby, significant to Station 2.

This double company, rescue and battalion station was the best of the best. They also had a rumored reputation of running off women, by either making them quit or sending them to another station. Later, that would be debunked as just talk, with me as the rookie facing those traditional challenges in the beginning of my profession. Okay ... I'll admit it: I was terrified, beyond terrified. At that very moment, I asked God why in the world He had placed me in a position like this. I would ask this question of God more than once. The first time was when I was about to ascend a seventy-five-foot aerial ladder, lock in on the very top, lean back, clap my hands in the air two times, and come back down—all in under two minutes. Just before I was to do this, I was told, "For the most part, this is safe to do." Piece of cake. Right? Looking straight ahead and only at each rung of the ladder, not looking up and not looking down, eyes front and forward, asking God each time I grabbed onto another rung, *Why? And what in the world am I doing here?*

The second time, it was déjà vu. I had to meet my nemesis again: that seventy-five-foot dragon fighter. The first time, unbeknownst to me at the time, it was safer. I had a rope attached to me, so if I forgot to lock in at the top and leaned back, or if anything went wrong, the rope would catch me and keep me from plummeting down. This time, there was no safety net or safety rope, nor a belay. Trying to hold back the tears, I sucked it up and did it, but be assured that as I headed up to the top, I asked God, once again, *Why?* It would take me seventeen years at that same department to maybe, just maybe, get the answer to that question.

Firefighters remember their first day. We also remember our first fire. And what a blunder that was for me. It was a working apartment fire, which means that the building and specific apartment units are actually involved with fire; the big "W" (frequently expressed). Flames were through the roof. My engine was first on the scene. I had the nozzle—every firefighter's desire, whether it is your first day or your last. You get that nozzle, and you don't let go. I had many guys swear to me they would give me the nozzle back, but I never gave it up. "Get your own; this one is mine," I'd tell them. Being first on the scene, first on nozzle, gave you bragging rights as part of the crew who knocked that fire down. I was ready, packed out with my turnout gear and air-pack on, breathing air.

My lieutenant and I got off the truck. I pulled my nozzle and extended the hose line perfectly, and then I ran to the door. He came from behind me, and he kicked the door open. (That was cool and impressive!) The room was clear. The fire alarm inside was so loud, I couldn't hear anything but heavy breathing leaving the portal of my mask. My heart was pounding with so much adrenaline, all I could do was catch my breath and hope I had it in me to fight that fire. I waited for my lieutenant to give the next command. Instead, he said a few choice cuss words and then added, "We are too far ahead of the fire." The next thing I heard him say was, "Hold on." And then he was gone. He left me there, inside the apartment. I was like, *Great. Now what. This is it?* It seemed like forever before he came back. But let me say this. When they teach you to stay on your hose line, you do it, because the system works: it will either lead you to the fire (or, in this case, firefighter) or to the fire truck. And they were right. My lieutenant came right back to me; he found me. But he was not happy. No, not happy at all. Because, apparently, what he had *actually* said was, "Come on," not "Hold on."

That was it. My glory day of proving myself was over, and my dream of being the rookie firefighter who knocked that fire down was gone. He moved to another location and placed me with the rescue crew to put out hot spots. That kept me out of his sight. He didn't speak to me for the rest of the shift. Fortunately, it wouldn't be long before we were dispatched on another fire, where I had the opportunity to redeem myself. As I sat on the ground recouping from that fire, my lieutenant came to me and said, "Good job."

My lieutenant taught me many things during the year that I spent at Station 2. One of those lessons was to discover the love I had for running. He knew women lacked upper body strength, but he rarely concerned himself with that issue. Instead, he focused on my endurance. He wanted me to be able to hang in there to the very end with the crew. It wasn't about what you could do on your own; it was what you could do as a team. Running was going to give me what I needed to be up to that task. As my strength and endurance increased, there were many instances when it would be time for a break to let a fresh crew in to fight the fire, but sometimes I was not ready to go out. I still had enough in me to go some more. I noticed the rest of the guys were the same way. The unspoken feeling was *Let's finish what we started; get it done.* Sometimes you could do that. Other times, you had to rotate; it was the safest thing to do.

My lieutenant also taught me the importance of nutrition and hydration while you rested up for another round. He always took the time to speak to me about anything; there was nothing that he was afraid to talk to me about. He also had a knack for reading people, and, for the most part, he was dead-on. The day he came to talk to me at the kitchen table he was dead-on. He noticed I wasn't a big eater. He questioned me about it. I had a fear of food. I thought that if I could just eat a little, enough to get by at supper time, I would be fine. Our officers had a rule about meals. There were many tasks that we would complete on our own, and you had free time when you could go to be by yourself while at the station. But, come breakfast and dinner, we all sat at the table together. There was no deviation from that at all. He noticed I didn't eat breakfast or lunch, and I only ate very little for supper. He was concerned, and we had a long talk about this. Well, he did most of the talking, and I did not admit one bit that I actually had a problem with food. This was a very bad risk that I was taking; not only for myself but also for my crew. It would be several years before I discovered that my eating disorder was a health risk that led to severe complications and consequences.

Anyway, I played a bit with running, built up my endurance, and then discovered that when I ran, I could eat and not have to worry too much about gaining weight. How cool was that! So, I ran. Later in my career, I was transferred to Station 12 ("Taj Mahal," as it was commonly called among firefighters). It was basically brand new and the largest station in Fulton County at that time. I found a track to use, so, in the morning before I work, I would run the track for about three to six miles every third day. And then I would do the same when I got off work the following morning. Sometimes I would just run the track. Other days, I would run the track, along with running up and down the stadium steps. But I started to notice that I was gaining weight. No matter how much I ran, or did not eat, I could not lose those extra five pounds. And I had no clue where that additional weight had come from. I weighed myself practically every day.

Not long after that, I got a call from my mother. She had just found out that she had hypothyroidism, and she suggested that I should get checked out. So, I made an appointment with the doctor. It was no surprise that I, too, was diagnosed with hypothyroidism. I was given twenty-five micrograms of Synthroid, a synthetic thyroid-hormone replacement drug that helps manage the symptoms associated with hypothyroidism. My doctor advised me that, by taking this medication, I should start seeing the extra weight come off. My problems were solved. Or were they?

Let's fast-forward a bit. Eight years later, Sandy Springs, John's Creek, and the city of Milton were no longer unincorporated cities of Fulton County. They were their own cities now, each with their own fire department. The firefighters who remained were sent to the south side of Fulton County to finish out their careers. I was reassigned to Station 17 after a temporary stay at Station 11. I started having a problem with diarrhea. Every time I ate, I found myself running to the bathroom. It wasn't until about nine months later that I realized there was a problem. We were having a live fire training day. I was at the nozzle, and it was my time to attack the fire. I was second in the rotation. For the very first time in my career, I had to drop out. I felt my muscles and my whole body slowly going into a complete collapse. My chief informed me I was white as a ghost. My blood pressure dropped to ninety over sixty. It took nearly the entire rest of the shift for my blood pressure to return to somewhat of a normal reading. At that point, I knew I had to go to the doctor to find out what was wrong with me.

A few weeks later, I was at my primary physician's office. There was very little he could do. He took some blood samples and referred me to a gastrointestinal (GI) specialist. She ordered more blood work, set up an appointment to have a colonoscopy performed, and then prescribed two forms of medication: a bulking agent for the diarrhea and a stool softener for when I became constipated from the bulking agent. In the meantime, my primary physician increased my Synthroid dosage, and I prepared myself for the colonoscopy.

The colonoscopy came back pretty much negative: a few polyps removed, and a small concern that the lining in my colon was changing. The GI specialist advised that she would continue with another procedure every one to two years to watch for any further changes in my condition. She wanted to follow up in two weeks to see how I was doing.

During my next visit, I brought some information to her attention. I had started doing my own research and noticed labels with the words "Gluten Free" on them. I was intrigued and wanted to find out more about this gluten—whatever it was. I discovered on the internet that people with gluten intolerances had most, if not all, of my symptoms: bloating, severe stomach pain after eating, painful diarrhea, nausea. These were just some of the problems I was experiencing. So, I started doing more research on gluten and found out it was in wheat, rye, and barley, and any products containing them. I eliminated gluten from my eating on a daily basis. I noticed that my symptoms had been reduced but not totally eliminated. My doctor was intrigued. With that information, she ordered an upper-GI endoscopy. She wanted to check me for celiac disease. So, I got ready for the next procedure. But there was a catch. I had to make myself sick in order for her to find the disease. I knew I was in for a long two weeks of pain and discomfort, and more diarrhea, because I had to allow my issues to return to get better test results.

The endoscopy went well. It was discovered that I had numerous, perhaps even as many as a hundred, pinhole ulcers in my stomach. The good news: no celiac. I was not happy. This placed me in a more discouraging situation; two procedures later, and still no real answers.

I knew something was wrong, and my condition was getting worse. The pain in my stomach when I ate became more excruciating, and there would be times when I would not even have enough time to make it to the bathroom. Many days would come and go, and I would thank God on those really bad and embarrassing days that I was alone. My doctor asked me if I was talking the medication she had prescribed. I told her I refused to take both medications—the bulking agent and laxatives—because this solved nothing; it only treated the symptoms, not the cause. What possible good result could come from a combination like that? I would take the bulking agent for the diarrhea and then the stool softener for the constipation, and then I was to the bulking agent. I couldn't see how this was a cure. All it did was cover up the problem and keep me on a continuing regimen of medication. This was something I was not going to settle for. I was not going to allow medication to rule my life. My doctor had increased my Synthroid to 250 micrograms. So, all I was doing was taking more medication, but I was not getting any better.

I continued to do more research. I found several websites related to celiac disease, autism, hyperactivity, and anxiety, just to mention a few. There were four contributing factors that stood out for me and my condition: gluten, corn, casein, and soy. If I had to eliminate these products, my first thought was *There goes the Mexican food*. But I had to do something; I was miserable. I was terrified. I now totally feared eating because I did not ever know when I would have to use the bathroom and how foods would affect me each time I ate. I always had to determine where the bathroom was before I sat down anywhere. I would go out to eat with a friend and be embarrassed about having to ask him to find a restroom three times before we finally made it back to my house. Sometimes I would have to leave the table just after having a few bites of my meal, leaving friends sitting at the table while I was gone for fifteen minutes, sometimes longer, during each bathroom visit. I did everything I could, including internet research, to find a way to solve my problem. Nothing worked, and if it did, it only worked for a very short time, and then I was back in the bathroom again. I was losing all confidence in my doctors—actually any doctors—and losing hope of finding a solution.

Now, back to the episode with my lymph nodes and the fear of lupus. Three or four doctors and two weeks later, more blood was drawn. Fourteen different vials of blood were taken from me. Again, nothing came up except that my B_{12} was low. The doctor accused me of not taking my Synthroid, again. I was told that I had mononucleosis (commonly known as mono). I rejected that result. Yes, I was exposed to it because my daughter had it, but that was not my problem. My symptoms were not a result of having mono. At this point, I was satisfied with nothing. No one was listening to me. They were treating the monitor and not the patient. This was one of the first things I was taught when I was attending class to become an emergency medical technician (EMT). Someone might be having a heart attack, but it doesn't show on the EKG monitor. So, you learn to listen to your patient and treat the person accordingly. I was exhausted, and I felt I was going to have to live with this—whatever it was—for the rest of my life, and no doctor could help me. And now I had to give myself B_{12} shots? Frustrated with not getting any closer to solving the problem, I made another change. I changed doctors. All of the them.

I took the advice of my captain and went to see his doctor. He reassured me his doctor would get to the bottom of it (no pun intended). I was eager to make the change. My first appointment was very hopeful. He actually listened to me. He sent me to two other places: the office of a GI specialist, for recommendations and tests, and the hospital, for an ultrasound for my thyroid, which he was concerned about because it was too large. He started me on a new program for my thyroid, just until he got the results of the blood work. I got a call two days later, and he referred me to an endocrinologist (a specialist who diagnoses and treats diseases that affect the glands, such as the thyroid). I started feeling hopeful.

In the meantime, I met with the new GI specialist. I brought him up to speed with all my medical problems that had occurred up to that point. For the first time, he gave me an answer to my problems. He told me I had IBS (irritable bowel syndrome). It did not matter what I ate; I was going to have bouts of diarrhea. He prescribed some pills for the acid in my stomach and a probiotic to get the good bacteria back into my system to help my digestive tract function a little better. I was relieved, to a point; finally, I had a name for my problem.

A friend had come to the doctor's office with me, and as we were leaving, he said, "Well, he said you can eat anything you want, and it doesn't matter. So, what do you want to eat?"

That was the easiest question to answer: Mexican food, of course.

For the next 3 weeks, I did just what the doctor said I could. I ate whatever I wanted. And I was miserable. I was exhausted the whole time, and my condition went from a little better to out of control. It was then that I knew this doctor was wrong. I could not eat whatever I wanted, and I had to figure something out fast. I met with my endocrinologist, and she gave me some insight that I thought was the breakthrough of my life. She recognized that I might have some malabsorption problem, and she prescribed Tirosint. This was the same medication as Synthroid but in a gel form. She started me on 125 micrograms, hoping the gel would absorb better than the pills, resulting in my thyroid performance increasing and my system getting back into a state of normal. Of course, I couldn't go to a doctor without him or her wanting my blood, so more blood work was done. But this time she asked for a different test: anti-TPO. She wanted to test the levels of my antithyroid peroxidase antibodies. She wanted to test my vitamin D and B_{12} as well. She scheduled me to see her again in about two weeks.

A few days later, I got a call from the endocrinologist's office informing me that the doctor called in a prescription for more B_{12}, which I was to take once a month. My vitamin D was borderline, so she would continue to monitor it. She diagnosed me as having Hashimoto's disease. I asked what that was, but her assistant didn't know. It sounded terrible. All I can remember asking is "What is that? What is that?" I could tell by her tone of voice that she had no idea what Hashimoto's was. How awkward to have to deliver a diagnosis when you did not even know what it was!

I was terrified. I was in tears. Just the name itself sounded so deadly. So, there I was, back on the computer, Google and I having it out on the screen, looking up each and every choice in the search results to help me find me the best information about this condition. And there is was on Wikipedia:

> Hashimoto's thyroiditis or chronic lymphocytic thyroiditis is an autoimmune disease in which the thyroid gland is attacked by a variety of cell- and antibody-mediated immune processes. It was the first disease to be recognized as an autoimmune disease.[1]
> It was first described by the Japanese specialist Hakaru Hashimoto in Germany in 1912.[2]

It wasn't *thyroid* that caught my eye. It was *autoimmune* that got me looking further into this whole ordeal of mine. Then, I found that all the diseases the doctors sought to diagnose me with were all also autoimmune diseases. Some factors and studies indicated that subjects who were diagnosed with lupus, celiac, and Crohn's also have developed Hashimoto's disease.

So, I looked even further and was shocked to discover I was on the right track. I had eliminated corn, gluten, soy, and casein. Why wasn't I getting better? What was I doing wrong? What could I do to get this under control and get myself better? I then discovered there weren't just four factors to eliminate, there were five. The fifth thing, which I

---

[1] Wikipedia, https://en.wikipedia.org/wiki/Hashimoto's_thyroiditis#cite_note-1.
[2] Yehuda Shoenfeld, Ricard Cervera, M. Eric Gershwin, *Diagnostic Criteria in Autoimmune Diseases* (Springer Science & Business Media, 2010, 216).

hadn't taken out of my diet, was sugar. Who would have thought that sugar, one of the most common food ingredients, could do so much harm to my body? This compound that is, after all, an ingredient in almost everything we buy and ingest.

By this time, I weighed 132 pounds. I was going to do anything I could to change that and beat my problem. So, I eliminated all five factors from my diet. My energy increased, my IBS went away, and I lost six pounds. I was literally no longer having to seek out the bathroom whenever I ate, and I felt my confidence in my progress increasing every day. I spoke with my endocrinologist, and she was impressed with my results. She encouraged me to continue with the great work. Before I left her office, she grounded me with the news that Hashimoto's is not reversible. Once again, I was pounded with bad news. The thought of having to live with this for the rest of my life, taking these pills every single day, was not an option. And, of course, I had to give more blood.

As I drove home from the doctor's office, I knew this could not be the end of my saga. I had come too far to accept these results and go down without another fight. Ask most of the people I know, and they will say that you don't tell me I can't do something. I will find a way to do it and make it work. Go until you get a no. But, in this situation, no was not an option. I worked on my own car because people told me I could not do it. That car had 306,000 miles on it before I sold it, and it is still on the road. It was only in an auto shop twice.

After research and more research, I came to the only conclusion that could very possibly fix my condition and the only thing that could truly help me: God and the Bible.

Chapter 2

The Autoimmune Disease

WHEN I FIRST THOUGHT there was a possibility that I had celiac, I really had no clue what this disease was and how it could impact me for the rest of my life. But it was not until lupus was knocking on my door, trying to rear its ugly face, that I realized all of these problems were classified into one disease. It was then that I took a further look and noticed that many sufferers diagnosed with one autoimmune disease (AD), actually had more than one disease connected to and classified as an AD. I was on a lupus forum and found that most people with lupus seemed to suffer with Crohn's, celiac, and Hashimoto's, but it was not just limited to these. The list of diseases that each one suffered with seemed to manifest into other problems, and the suffering seemed to have no end, as if there was a snowball effect. It appeared to be a no-win situation for anyone who became a victim of these terrible diseases, and all those diagnosed would most definitely suffer for the rest of their lives and literally die trying to find cures.

The research was endless, and the information was vast and overwhelming, with not just the disease itself but also everything I came across. There was one thing for sure: each year, more and more people suffered with these diseases. There are at least eighty diseases classified under AD, including rheumatoid arthritis (RA), Crohn's, rheumatic fever, diabetes, lupus, celiac, just to mention a few. Within this list, the diseases are classified as either accepted or suspected as AD. The ones mentioned above are actually accepted and classified as AD. The suspected ones may surprise you as much as they did me: endometriosis, multiple sclerosis (MS), and restless leg syndrome, again just to mention a few.[3, 4] In order for a disease to be classified as AD, it has to go through specific testing that answers Witebsky's postulates, a formula created by Ernst Witebsky and his colleagues in 1957, then later modified in 1994.[5]

But what is AD, and how can it affect so many people without even being contagious? The bubonic plague—the Black Death—that swept through Europe in the fourteenth century killed an estimated 25 million people.

Diseases do not have to be contagious to wipe out a community or more. According to the International Diabetes Federation, there are approximately 425 million people living with diabetes. By the year 2045, that is expected to rise as much as 629 million. 4 million deaths were caused by diabetes in 2017 with 212 million (1 in 2) people with diabetes were undiagnosed. 352 million in the same year were at risk of developing type 2. In a nutshell, one adult out of ten will have diabetes by 2030. And that is just one statistic for one disease. Gluten intolerance is on the rise with those who suffer with celiac.

---

[3] Wikipedia, List of Autoimmune Diseases, https://en.wikipedia.org/wiki/List_of_autoimmune_diseases.

[4] American Autoimmune Related Diseases Association, Inc, Autoimmune Disease List, https://www.aarda.org/diseaselist/.

[5] Scribd, Autoimmune Disease, https://www.scribd.com/document/145010667/Autoimmune-Disease.

It is estimated that 1 in every 160 adults has a gluten allergy in the United States. Approximately 544,000 people suffer from an irritable bowel disorder (IBD), which includes Crohn's; 100,000 new cases are reported each year. Approximately 700,000 visits to doctors' offices are attributed to IBD on an annual basis. I could continue with more statistics, but I feel I have made my point. These diseases are on the rise, and they are not stopping.

The most recent outbreak of the bubonic plague was reported in Madagascar, in 2008. Eighteen were reported dead. That is a far cry from the 25 million who died in fourteenth-century Europe. Although eighteen is a manageable number, it is still a threat in some countries. The first reported outbreak was in Egypt, in 1650–1550 BC, which was thought to be either bubonic plague or influenza. Diabetes and Crohn's also date back to the same era. Similar findings of symptoms had been reported, but placing a name to these symptoms did not follow until much later. Both and all are diseases, just as both and all are sure killers. Diabetes is rated seventh on the list of top-ten killer diseases of Americans. How is it that one disease can be controlled, but not the other? What keeps these diseases on the rise?

It has become common knowledge that the bubonic plague is an infection of the lymph glands (lymphatic system), caused by small rodents and their fleas. Later, a treatment of antibiotics became effective in treating this deadly infection. Cut and dried. They discovered where the disease originated from, found the cure, and, throughout the years, outbreaks were reduced; therefore, fewer people were affected, and most who were sickened and treated survived. Treatment within twenty-four hours of the first symptom meant that death could be prevented. So, what is different from this disease than the others? How could this disease be controlled when others could not? Again, to find the answers, I had to research where these diseases came from, how they originated, and, basically, what happened to start an epidemic of these chronic life-threatening ADs.

As with the plague, I needed to know where these ADs had originated and what had changed to afflict so many people. Now, with the bubonic plague, we knew it came from rats—well, rather, the fleas on the rats. The fleas carried the disease; so, when the rodent, be it a rat or a mouse, died, the fleas had to find another host in order to live. Although there where earlier outbreaks of bubonic plague among humans, notably during the sixth century, I wanted to focus more on the infamous outbreak in 1347: the one known as the Black Death. It began in China and spread to Italy, from where it then spread throughout other European countries. The rats that carried these fleas were transported back and forth from the ships during the exporting and importing of merchandise between the trading countries. So, a consequence to improved transportation and the ability to travel between these countries was the beginning of not only importing goods but also transporting diseases. Today, more precautions are taken to prevent such epidemics form happening again.

With AD I saw a greater challenge. This research would not be that cut and dried. I had to look more closely at the earlier years of research to find the nearly exact moment when things changed and this rash of chronic diseases started. Looking through time lines of many diseases, I chose just a few to compare to my research. Diabetes was my first comparison. The year 1552 BC is believed to mark the first discovery of documentation referring to symptoms that could be diabetes. This later came to be the discovery of type 1 diabetes, which is usually found in juveniles and/or young adults. It is an autoimmune destruction of the pancreas, which prevents the organ from producing insulin to break down sugars in the bloodstream. By AD 1500, and through 1670, there would be hundreds of authors writing about diabetes. But it was around AD 500 that the first descriptions of "sugar in the urine" and its occurrence in obese individuals would be documented. In 1500 BC, found on Ebers Papyrus (a 110-page scroll of ancient Egyptian medicine, the oldest preserved medical documents),[6] sugar in the urine also described as a condition that

6   Steve Neander, "Against the Grain," *A History of Diabetes* (timeline) (blog), June 29, 2006, http://neander-steve.blogspot.com/2006/06/history-of-diabetes-timeline.html.

resembled that of today's RA. The term lupus was first used and attributed to the thirteenth century, which gave a description of facial rashes that were markings similar to a wolf; hence, the Latin word *lupus*, meaning "wolf." As with many other diseases, MS existed long before it had a name, dating back to the Middle Ages, which lasted from the fifth century through the fifteenth.[7] Then, there were inflammatory bowel diseases (including Crohn's), which began to be discovered in the seventeenth century. We would be well into the twentieth century before most or all of these diseases described in earlier years would have names—some weren't named until the twenty-first century—and, later, to discover that they were all somewhat similar, because they would all be labeled ADs.[8]

These ADs occur when your body begins to attack itself, thinking it is a "foreign-like" object or substance it must get rid of, kind of like "friendly fire." The body sees it as the enemy and attacks. Our bodies are perfectly designed and structured down to every cell and its smallest trace of minerals. Everything in the body is designed to perform a particular function and has its own healing mechanisms. Why would it want to hurt itself and create such a mass destruction inside? What message was delivered improperly, and who sent it? Most, or at least some, researchers have proposed that the small intestines maybe the source of this haywire functioning and your body receiving that "mailer daemon" message.[9], [10]

The small intestines are primarily the source of where foods are broken down for the body to obtain the nutrients needed to function

---

[7]   Loren A Rolak, M.D., "The History of MS" (brochure), September 2015, https://www.nationalmssociety.org/NationalMSSociety/media/MSNationalFiles/Brochures/Brochure-History-of-Multiple-Sclerosis.pdf.

[8]   Daniel J Mudler, Angela J Noble, Christopher J. Justinich, Jcaclyn M. Duffin, "The Tale of Two diseases: The History of Inflammatory Bowel Disease," *Journal of Crohn's and Colitis*, May 1, 2014, https://academic.oup.com/ecco-jcc/article/8/5/341/616781.

[9]   Healthline.com, https://www.healthline.com/health/autoimmune-disorders.

[10] Amy Myers, MD, "Understanding the True Cause of Autoimmune Disease," amymyersmd.com, https://www.amymyersmd.com/2017/01/understanding-true-cause-autoimmune-disease/.

properly on a daily basis. Only the good stuff is supposed to get out and feed the body and organs. If the system fails and the small intestines are damaged, the major barrier that is within the intestinal pathway and lining the digestive tract will fail, and more than just the good and important nutrients get into our bloodstream and the rest of our system. Think of your intestines as a well-maintained garden hose. When the hose is properly cared for, water goes from the supply line to the end of the opening, and then the water flows out to where it should go. If left unattended and not properly cared for, the garden hose will deteriorate, and several small holes, and even larger holes, will be created, resulting in the water dispersing in several areas and not where it is intended to go. The most extreme result is possible chaos: water goes everywhere, and less reaches the end of the hose. With your intestines, more bad bacteria are dispersed throughout your body, and less nutrients are filtered and absorbed, creating less waste to be expelled from your body. If this happens, you get what some researchers link to acute and chronic diseases, such as diabetes and IBD. This intestinal hyperpermeability is also known as the "leaky gut syndrome." Your leaking gut begins to allow toxins, undigested foods, waste, or larger-than-normal macromolecules into your body. Once the out-of-place substances enter the GI system, the body will be affected directly and/or an immune reaction will be initiated.[11, 12]

So, now we know what is happening. How did it happen? What changed the human body to make it respond in such a way that it begins to "hurt itself"—a long, chronic journey of suicide, if you will. Once again, I am back into the history books. I knew that most of the ADs were beginning to be documented in and near the sixteenth century. So, I went back each year to see what significant change had occurred that could give me some kind of indication as

[11] Daniel J Mudler, Angela J Noble, Christopher J. Justinich, Jcaclyn M. Duffin, "The Tale of Two Diseases: The History of Inflammatory Bowel Disease," *Journal of Crohn's and Colitis*, May 1, 2014, https://academic.oup.com/ecco-jcc/article/8/5/341/616781.

[12] Healthline.com, https://www.healthline.com/health/autoimmune-disorders.

to what brought on these chronic diseases. The fifteenth century was the time of Joan of Arc, but nothing else really stood out. So, I went further back. The fourteenth century caught my eye; a lot happened during that century. Of course, there was the Black Death in 1347, the Great Famine of 1315, and the start of the Hundred Years' War. Leonardo da Vinci and Michelangelo were emerging artists in this new era, contributing to a new cultural movement. The Renaissance (the meaning of which is "rebirth; to be reborn"), a movement that spanned the period from the fourteenth century to the seventeenth, with the year 1325 often given as the onset. It was the change from the Middle Age to the Modern Age. It changed everything, and everything changed with it.

Even before the Renaissance began, eating habits were poor in the Middle Ages (also known as the Dark Ages). Nobles and the wealthy ate mostly meat, with very few vegetables; most of the time, fruits were found in pies or preserved in honey. Vegetables and fruit were mostly eaten by the poor. Dairy products and most vegetables were deemed to be inferior foods and were not placed on a noble's table; only onions, garlic, and leeks would possibly be found at mealtimes for the noble and wealthy. Good hygiene was not a high priority back then either, which may have been a leading cause of deteriorating health back then for some, if not most, people. So, in addition, since eating habits were poor, it would be no surprise to find symptoms of diabetes throughout those centuries. This is only the beginning; there is more to come.

Now we come to the Renaissance. With overseas traveling in place, new foods and culinary influences were introduced. The desire for change increased, and it became ever more popular to have access to these new foods and learn how to cook them. Even back then, there were people trying to warn against these new ways. The rights and wrongs of eating, how foods should be eaten and combined appropriately, and so on. (I'm in awe of how some things do remain the same.) Thomas Cogan's *The Haven of Health* (1584) and Thomas Moffett's *Health's Improvement* (1655) are among the writings that began to warn people of frugal and moderate eating.[13], [14] Despite the warnings, a tradition from the Middle Ages carried on: in general, meat and fish were considered to be more nourishing and healthier than fruits and vegetables. So, these foods were eaten in abundance; cookbooks were written to inspire others to prepare the perfect peacock and other large game birds. Warnings from dietitians continued to warn about the dangers of these foods.

In the first fifty years of the sixteenth century, a royal, noble, or wealthy family could consume "900 tons of wheat; 100 tons of pulses or dried, edible seeds of the legume family; 234,000 gallons of wine; 60 tons of beef and veal; 40 tons of fish; 15,000 fowls; 6 tons of salted meat; 4 tons of cheese; 3,086 pounds of butter; 2,204 pounds of ricotta cheese. All was eaten by a range of 500 to 750 people or courtiers." All prepared by a progressed professional cook, who, of course, had to present himself with the "lack of filth and dirt and had to have the knowledge of fish, meats, and vegetables and understand what should be roasted, boiled, or fried, and utilize spices so as not to have anything too salty or flat."[15]

The discovery of the New World brought new foods and different culinary practices, including the potato and corn. In the latter half of the fifteenth century, Columbus and other explorers of the Americas, Asia, and Africa brought back tobacco, coffee, tea, and chocolate.[16] They were meant to be for medicinal purposes, but, later, were added to the dietary routines of early modern Europe. Then, around 1560, sugar was introduced. By the eighteenth century, sugar consumption exploded from four pounds per year in the 1700s to around eighteen

[13] Sidney Lee, Moffeett, Thomas, *Dictionary of National Biography, 1885–1900,* volume 38, Wikisource, January 30, 2011, https://en.wikisource.org/wiki/Moffett,_Thomas_(DNB00).

[14] George Eric Simpson, "The Haven of Health," *The Scientific Monthly* 10, no. 1 (1920): 26–37, http://www.jstor.org/stable/6886.

[15] Castles and Manor Houses, Food, http://www.castlesandmanorhouses.com/life_04_food.htm.

[16] James T. Ehler, "Food History Timeline 1600 to 1625", foodreference.com, http://www.foodreference.com/html/html/food-history-1600.html.

pounds per year by the first decade of the nineteenth century.[17] Today, in the twenty-first century, Americans consume ninety-five to one hundred pounds of sugar each year, per person, according to the *New York Times* (October 28, 2012, in the Business Day section of the newspaper). So, with the explosion of sugar production, the invention of dessert made it into the mid-seventeenth century. The savory sweet revolution took a front seat to the old strong-flavored and heavily spiced sauces and condiments. These sweet dishes became an added addition to the course of meals. Some health experts claimed these dishes were unnatural. But this unnatural dish added to the market a new craftsman: the confectioner. He made sour things sweet, preserved all fruits, and was an architect of all desserts. By the eighteenth century, the abundance of food supplied in one setting became an impressive event. The nobles' tables commonly had five dishes: pig, meat, and greens, fowl, beef, mutton, veal, and lamb comprised one course; venison, fowl, or fish made up another; last of all was pudding (dessert in the US). To drink there was beer made with molasses, wine, and English beer, along with liquor.[18, 19, 20]

It is amazing how things get completely reversed. In the beginning, God said in Genesis 1:29 (NIV), "I give you every seed-bearing plant on the face of the whole earth and every tree has fruit with seed in it. They will be yours for food."[21] And in what seemed to be the blink of an eye, we went from consuming fruits and vegetables to eating mostly meat. Later, the destruction of the soil hindered

[17] Kamila Sitwell, "Typical Sugar Consumption Now vs. 100 Years Ago," divineatingout.com, November 21, 2016, http://www.divineeatingout.com/food-1/sugar-consumption-now-vs-100-years-ago.

[18] "Food in the Renaissance—Renaissance Time!" Google Sites, https://sites.google.com/a/mycsla.org/renaissance-today/home/food-in-the-renaissance.

[19] Lindsey Green, and Alex Hollis. "Food in the Renaissance—Renaissance Quest," Google Sites, https://sites.google.com/a/mycsla.org/renaissance-quest/renaissance-stuff/food-in-the-renaissance.

[20] "Jane Austen's World," Jane Austen's World, November 26, 2009, https://janeaustensworld.wordpress.com/tag/food-in-the-regency-era/.

[21] Genesis 1:29 NIV, Bible Gateway, https://www.biblegateway.com/passage/?search=Genesis 1:29&version=NIV.

the minerals and nutrients intended for growth of all plants, and then pesticides caused further damage. The production of processed foods and the mills built to process these foods created a no-win situation for our bodies. Our digestive system could not change and was not designed to evolve with the changes to the environment. So, it suffered and broke down, and all the organs soon became affected. Now millions are suffering and dying from the resulting conditions. These are just added factors to the main problem. The reality is that what you eat today can very well affect the health of your children, your grandchildren, and even your great-grandchildren. Two genetic studies concluded that a diet, be it poor or healthy, can alter the nature of one's DNA, and those changes can be passed on to descendants. These findings could quite possibly explain the increased genetic risk that children face, compared to their parents, in terms of obesity and diabetes, among others. I even think that this is also the cause of why more and more women are discovering they are infertile, with no medical explanation given to them.

So, the reason for all these ADs is not just from the current conditions of today. They could very well be the result of how our ancestors ate, and the altered DNA has been passed on from generation to generation, with the result of millions now affected. That doesn't include those walking around who do not even know that they have an AD. Can this be changed? Can we fix this? Is there any possible chance that these diseases can be reversed, even to the extent that our unborn children, and their children, would have a chance for healthier and possibly disease-free lives?

I believe … yes, it is possible! Sometimes, the past holds the key to the present.

Chapter 3

The Meat Eater versus the Vegetarian

I HAVE COME ACROSS A lot of variances when it comes to what is best for the body, including whether to have meat in your diet or embrace the life of a naturalist, vegetarian, or a vegan. As I looked further into the choices, I found that this can become a very controversial subject and/or debate; therefore, I have placed myself in an unbiased conclusion of what I think is best for both lifestyles.

I have discovered and heard that many doctors will advise their patients to cut down on red meat intake for health purposes, such as reducing cholesterol and lowering high blood pressure. This has become a common tactic that has proved itself, time after to time, to be very effective. Eating less red meat also reduces other risks, such as bowel cancer, Alzheimer's disease, osteoporosis, arthritis, heart disease, and breast cancer, just for starters. My first lieutenant told me that he was once a meat eater, and his doctor advised him that his cholesterol was high; he needed to reduced his meat intake and take medication to reduce the plaque building in his arteries. He didn't just reduce his meat intake; he cut it out altogether. By doing this, he lowered his cholesterol, and is no longer on any medication. Reducing red meat in the diet works, and it is a great benefit to most people. Yet, there are also great benefits to eating red meat. It's a good source of zinc, iron, potassium, magnesium, selenium, and B vitamins, not to mention that it is the most common source everyone seeks as a complete protein. All or some good-tasting meats can contribute to a healthy immune system and even weight loss, if based on a high-protein diet. So, what is the "beef" on meat? Is meat really that bad for us? Or, was it given to us by God to be used for nourishment, and have we caused it to be bad for us?

God clearly stated on the sixth day of creation, in Genesis 1:29, "Behold I have given you every herb bearing seed, which {is} upon the face of the earth, and every tree, in which {is} the fruit of a tree yielding seed; to you it shall be for meat." It shall be "meat," or food; this is a pretty good start or ending for a vegetarian to seal his or her win in a debate on this subject. There it is in a nutshell; nothing else to debate. But, as you read further into the Bible, there are changes to the story, and new instructions arise. Genesis 9:3 tells us that God said, "Every moving thing that liveth shall be meat for you; even as the green herb I have given you all things." So, what happened? Did God change his mind? God doesn't change, but people do.

God Is an Animal-Rights Activist ... a Big One

If you recall, Adam and Eve were both vegetarians. Even the animals were vegetarians. We read in Genesis 1:30, "And to every beast of the earth and to every bird of the heavens and to everything that creeps on the earth, everything that has the breath of life, I have given every green plant for food." It was not till after the flood that God allowed the animals to be consumed as meat and provided enough of them for that purpose. So, is it possible that God really intended for us to be vegetarians? In Leviticus 17:13–14, God speaks to Moses, commanding, "Whatever man of the children of Israel or of strangers who dwell among you, Who hunts and catches any animal or bird that may be eaten, he shall pour out its blood and cover it with dust. For it is the life of all flesh. Its blood sustains its life … ." God didn't change His mind; He just had to set new standards.

In our "fallen state," did humans desire to eat meat, giving rise to God having to make provisions for us to eat meat? Would this now be considered a commandment or a concession? In order to determine which it is, you must first define *concession*. We read in 1 Corinthians 7:6–9, "But I say this as a concession, not as a commandment. For I wish that all men were even as I myself. But each one has his own gift from God, one in this manner and another in that. But I say to the unmarried and to the widows: It is good for them if they remain even as I am, but if they cannot exercise self-control, let them marry. For it is better to marry than to burn with passion." A *concession*, according to *Merriam-Webster's Dictionary*, is "something done or agreed to usually grudgingly in order to reach an agreement or improve a situation." God, obviously, would prefer us to solely be as one with Him, but he knows our hearts and desires, and should you not have the ability to control those desires, then it is better to marry and still be pleasing to and honor God. So, would it come to pass that before the flood and after man fell, humans had a desire to eat animals? It could be possible that from the wickedness and evil that was among those of the land, some could have begun killing the animals to eat their meat; therefore, God had to protect the animals, which needed to fear man in order to survive.

I believe that before the fall of man, there was no fear within the animals or humans. Fear was established, and awareness of Adam and Eve's nakedness only occurred after eating from the Tree of Knowledge. You only get word of eating meat after the flood, when God established his covenant with Noah and changed the order of things from the way He had originally established them in the Garden of Eden. It was a new beginning, another fresh start, with some changes added to it. He created the food chain and the balance of all in earth and in heaven. With that balance, new standards had to be set, and one of them was not eating flesh or blood, because blood represented life. As long as the blood still flowed through the veins, the animal is still alive. God did not want the animals eaten alive, and with the fear of man in the animals, their chances of survival increased. Proverbs 12:10 states, "A righteous man regards the life of his animal, But the tender mercies of the wicked are cruel." You will even find that on the seventh day, God commanded the cattle to rest (Exodus 20:10). Animal cruelty should not even be an issue if we are commanded to be the caretakers or stewards over everything that God made, and we are to protect and take care of them in any way we can. Are we not responsible? Is it not our job to make sure disease and sickness remain under control? That means controlling the numbers, but it should also mean preventing too many from being killed and any from being abused.

So, where is our self-control? Where do you draw the line to eat or not eat meat? As 1 Timothy 4:4 states, "For every creature of God is good ..." God laid down the guidelines for eating meat, and He also gave us the means to eat meat. But the way animal meats are now mass produced, with the animals fed in a manner in which they were not meant to be fed, and kept and contained in cruel ways, reflect actions are tender mercies of the wicked and not ways in which God is glorified. There are many documentaries on the cruel and inhumane ways cows and chickens, and even pigs, are treated and killed brutally for food and for profit; and let us not forget the killing of animals for sport. There are companies that feed and maintain proper care for all the animals; it is up to us to try to use these companies to purchase our meats. Doing proper research, reading labels, and also talking with your butcher will give you all the information you need to make the right choices as to which meat to bring home for you and your family. Look for organic, free range, no antibiotics, no preservatives added, minimally processed. Most food markets are allowing for easier access to the kind of products that show care and compassion to the livestock. Although halal and kosher meats represent one of the most humane methods of animal slaughter, that does not mean the meat is organic or without additives and preservatives. They are simply foods that can be consumed according to Islamic and Jewish religious laws because the animals were slaughtered in a ritually proper manner.

God provided certain instructions for preparing meat that was to be eaten, specifically for the chosen Israelites. And if those guidelines were not met, then you did not eat the meat. So, many people adhered to those rules. You could purchase meat at the market, but if you were unsure if it was prepared in a means that honored and glorified God, then those who kept kosher chose not to eat it. This also prevented them from eating meat that was used for sacrifices. These specifications also may have prevented them from consuming any disease or contamination that was in the blood of the animal. Again, blood is a symbol of life; to honor the life of the animal, the blood had to be completely let out of the animal's body and then covered with dirt or dust, if you will. This also prevented animals from being eaten while still alive. And, most of all, it was all designed to glorify God and to assure glorification of Him in all things, including eating.

Then, God laid out other special instructions for only certain animals to be eaten. This, too, was designed for the Israelites so that they could be recognized as the "Chosen People." There were special laws and provisions required by God so that others would know who they were and recognize them as such. Throughout history, various groups of people have considered themselves to be the chosen people of God, for a purpose. Most of these religions are traced back to their common origin of Abraham, involving approximately 54 percent of the world's population. With these specifications, we have the products that are created to conform ritually: either kosher (of the Jewish religion) or halal (of the Islamic religion). Both share the same meaning of "permitted" or "lawful," when translated, and they are popular traditions still maintained and practiced today.

In conclusion, when pondering whether to eat meat or not to eat meat, eat the meat. If it was a concession, God would have said it was a concession. It is not a commandment either. I think, it is a choice. In the beginning, all things were pure. No evil, no sin, no death, no fear. The animals did not fear man; nor did man fear animals. Yes, I do believe that in the beginning, we were created to be vegetarians, and so were the animals. We were also created to be without sin. With that, He instilled in us all free will and choice, and when a choice was made to eat from the forbidden Tree of the Knowledge of Good and Evil, well, that was when man fell. So, with that, everything changed. All things became corrupt, so God set out to destroy it all. He instructed Noah to build an ark to save the righteous, in Genesis, chapter 6. Save two animals of each species; other food was gathered to feed Noah and his family and the animals. After the flood, everything had changed even more. Now there was a food chain. We now feared animals, and they now feared us. In Genesis 9:2–3, God blesses Noah and his sons and tells them, "And the fear of you and the dread of you shall be on every beast of the earth and on every fowl of the air, upon all that moveth upon the earth and upon all the fishes of the sea. They are given into your hand. Every moving thing that lives shall be food for you. I have given you all things, even the green herbs." This is the first time that God grants that meat can be eaten, but with the restriction that it has to be killed first. We can speculate all day long as to why God allowed the animals to be used as food, but He did, and it is not until Leviticus, chapter 11, that we find restrictions of certain animals, including the prohibition of fat and blood. (Again, these were instructions for the Israelites.) God clearly states the animals that are permitted and forbidden, including but not limited to pork and rabbit, camel, and seafood without fins and scales. A suggestion of being not clean and uneatable. (Remember, this message was sent from God through Moses to the children of Israel. He then repeats this command in Deuteronomy, chapter 14.)

As we move further into the Bible, we come to the New Testament, when Jesus Christ walks the earth among us and brings new commandments and laws for us to obey by. In Acts 10:1–48, Peter has his vision, starting with verse 9:

> About noon the following day as they were on their journey and approaching the city, Peter went up

on the roof to pray. [10] Then he became hungry and wanted something to eat, but while they made ready, he fell into a trance. [11] and saw heaven opened and an object like a great sheet bound at the four corners, descending to him and let down to the earth [12] In it were all kinds of four-footed animals of the earth, wild beasts, creeping things, and birds of the air.[13] Then a voice came to him, "Rise, Peter. Kill and eat." [14] But Perter said, Not so Lord! For I have never eaten anything common or unclean." [15] And the voice spoke to him again, "What God has cleansed you must not call common." [16] This was done three times, and the object was taken up into heaven again.

Let's repeat these two verses. "Rise Peter kill and eat. What God has cleansed you must not call common." In 1 Timothy 4:4–5, we read, "For every creature of God is good and nothing is to be refused if it is received with thanksgiving, for it is sanctified by the word of God and prayer." This is true, whether you eat only vegetables or you include meat in your meal. God is perfectly fine with either or both. One person's faith or choice may allow them to eat anything, but another, who eats only vegetables, is not weak in faith and has the choice to make that decision on their own. [3] " For one believeth that he may eat all things: another, who is weak, eateth herbs. Let not him that eateth despise him that eateth not; and let not; him which eateh not judge him that eateth: for God hath received him" (Romans 14:2–3 KJV). Here, the apostle Paul gives us the ability to choose, but cautions us to not judge others who chose differently from us. Eat the meat and eat the vegetables; it does not matter how you eat them, together or alone. Do it for the glory of God. When we give praise and thanks to Him for all things that are received, they will be made holy. God is good, and the meat is good; the animals were given to us to care for and to be used as food. Just remember, all things belong to God, as 1 Corinthians 8:8 tells us, "But food does not commend us to God, for neither if we eat are we better, nor if we do not eat are the worse." God has provided us with all these things, including His covenant, and He has not broken one promise. We are the ones who have misused all things provided by God. By honoring Him through our praise and thanks, by taking care of those things that He has given us, including all the creatures, we give the glory to Him. Remember, food will not bring you closer to God, but glorifying Him and praying to Him will.

So, now that is has been established that meat is an intended food source, How much is enough? Let's be clear on one thing: it is obvious and should be very clear to everyone that we do not need to eat meat to survive or maintain a healthy lifestyle. Meat is one of the major compacted food groups in the food-guide pyramid. Many of the same nutrients found in meat can be found in foods like eggs, dried beans, and nuts. We choose to eat meat, and, therefore, we must accept that this choice comes with risks, especially with the overconsumption of meat. More than 80 percent of the protein in the average American's diet comes from meat, according to the 2010 Dietary Guidelines for Americans. One ounce of meat is equal or equivalent to one once of protein; according to the US Department of Agriculture, it is recommended that you consume no more than approximately four ounces of total meat per day to meet the protein recommendations. But you need to be aware that some meat choices are going to be better than others. For example, some cuts of red meat contain higher amounts of unhealthy fats—saturated fats that can increase your LDL (or "bad") cholesterol levels. Fatty fish, on the other hand, contain healthy fats. Based on the recommendations by the USDA, no more than 1.8 ounces of red meat, 1.5 ounces of poultry, and 0.4 ounces of seafood should be consumed on a daily basis, so the rest of your protein should be obtained from other nonmeat sources, such as nuts and beans and eggs, which can be just as healthy.

When you consume protein, your body breaks it down into amino acids. The human body can produce ten of the twenty amino acids, so the remaining ten must be obtained from food. This organic compound is needed for the body to break down food, grow, and repair body tissue; amino acids are also essential for many other body functions. Amino acids make up 75 percent of the human body and have become a key component for body builders. Amino acids are classified into three groups: essential, nonessential, and conditional. The nonessentials are the amino acids that your body produces even if they are not obtained from food. The essential acids cannot be produced by the body; therefore, they must come from a food source. The conditionals are usually not essential except in times of illness and stress. Your body does not store essential amino acids, and therefore it is necessary to obtain the protein for the compound on a daily basis. Studies show that the best way to get these essential amino acids is by the consumption of meat and eggs. For vegetarians, it is difficult to obtain all the amino acids on a daily basis through just beans and nuts, because these only have a portion of the essentials. Soy has been labeled a complete protein source for vegetarians to use to maintain the essential amino acids needed to sustain a healthy lifestyle.

We are a nation of meat eaters, there is no doubt. In 2011, according to the USDA, a total of 25.6 billion pounds of US beef was consumed. In cattle and calf production, that equates to meat sales of about $45.2 billon. On average, Americans purchase an estimated two hundred pounds of meat per year, which would bring the daily intake of meat to nine ounces per day. That is more than what the USDA recommends. Although the USDA has reported that the amount of meat purchased between 1930 and 2007 had nearly doubled, studies show that from 2007 to 2011, it seemed that Americans were buying less meat, approximately 12 percent less. But, as a whole, Americans still consume way too much meat, exceeding daily recommendations. This is not something that began in the 1930s. The habit of eating too much meat has been going on since before the Renaissance, if you recall chapter 2. The results prove themselves, with diabetes on the rise, and high cholesterol, high blood pressure, and obesity all getting out of control.

I must confess, I was one of those Americans in the USDA report. I was a huge meat eater. There was nothing tastier than a filet mignon or ribeye cooked medium rare and seasoned with special salts and pepper, with a baked potato on the side. The steak was tender and juicy, melting in my mouth with every single bite. I would always be asked if I wanted steak sauce with my meal when it was served. I took and ate my steak with seriousness. I was a firm believer that all a good piece of meat needed was salt and pepper and a hot grill, cooked four to six minutes on each side. So, my reply, in the same soft yet threatening voice, was always "I better not need that sauce." It was a guaranteed meal that I knew would not hurt me, but it *was* hurting me; I just didn't know it. I will be the first to admit I overly consumed all the meat I ate: red meat, fish, and chicken.

The chicken— oh my goodness, what happened to the chicken? This should be a concern as well. Although it is a better choice, how can you choose chicken, knowing how they are raised, caged, and fed with food that makes them so fat, they can't even walk? A cage-free chicken is a happy chicken, so we are supposed to just eat happy chickens and happy eggs and know we are making a better choice in our eating habits. Come on, people, I am nowhere near a vegetarian, but a happy chicken is one that is still on the range, not on your plate. It boils down to knowing who is raising and producing your food. Watch documentaries, and read all the labels. Do your research, and know what it is that you are actually putting into your body. Finding the smallest chicken in a place that thrives on organic or cares for such practices as halal or kosher may provide you with a head start on preparing a healthier meal for you and your family. There are several documentaries[22] I watched to help me be aware so that I could make better choices. You have a choice; you have the ability to find the truth. Don't just stop here with this book. Find all the information you can, and shop and buy where you can get the best quality of food, not the best quantity.

A healthy diet consists of carbohydrates, fats, and proteins, to reduce the risk of diabetes and other health complications. You can

---

[22] Food, Inc. Forks over Knives, Supersize Me, Simply Raw, GMO OMG.

calculate how much protein you need based on how many calories you take in on a daily basis, or how many calories you need to take in to reach your desired weight. By the end of this book, you will have all the information needed to be able to calculate the right amount for all your nutritional needs. There are several ways you can obtain this information. You can Google a protein calculator, which gives you the information based on the data it asks for, such as your age and height. A Canadian study determined that sedentary people should consume 0.86 grams of protein per kilogram of weight, moderately active people should consume 1.40 grams per kilogram of weight, and professional athletes should consume 2.54 grams of protein. I myself am old school and prefer the older method of calculating my protein intake. I keep up with the amount of calories I am eating, so I base my protein intake on how many calories I am allowing myself for that day. I eat, on average, 1,200 calories a day, so I figure 10 to 15 percent of my daily calories will come from my protein sources. So, my daily diet should include 120 to 180 calories from protein. Since four calories are equal to one gram of protein, my protein intake should be thirty to forty-five grams.

When I am not counting calories, I figure my intake based on my weight. I take my weight in pounds, then divide it by 2.2 to get my weight in kilograms. I then multiply my weight in kilograms by 0.8 (not active) and up to 1.8 if exercising. My weight of 115 pounds, divided by 2.2, equals 52.27 kilograms. Multiplying 52.27 times 0.8, equals 41 grams of protein. There is not that much difference when calculating using the 1.8 figure.

Below are just a few examples of how much protein you can obtain in certain foods; the meat is based on an average of one hundred grams, or three ounces, of meat, with the exception of beef, which is six ounces. The vegetables will range from a half-cup to one-cup serving.

Meat	Protein	Vegetables	Protein
Chicken	30g	Broccoli	1.86g
Fish	26g	Sweet Potato	2.29g
Pork Loin	28g	Carrots	0.59g
Beef (lean)	42g	Celery	1.25g
Tofu	7g	Beans	17.00g
Eggs	13g	Eggplant	0.82g
Yogurt/Milk	8g	Corn	4.02g
Nuts/Seeds	22g	Kale	2.47g
Cheese	32g	Okra	3.00g
Lamb	23g	Potato	4.33g
		Swiss Chard	3.29g

For a more complete list of healthy alternatives for your daily intake of protein, you can go to www.health-alternatives.com. There, you will find more choices of vegetables and the listings of the protein each vegetable contains. The more options you have, the higher the chances are that you will make better choices for a healthier lifestyle.

Remember to make the best and healthiest choices when it comes to eating protein. Try to get most of your protein from your vegetables, whenever possible. The plants that have all the essential amino acids are algae, amaranth, buckwheat, hemp, soybeans, and quinoa. If your choice is meat, choose the leanest and most minimally processed types, and you can include an ounce of cheese to get the most of your daily protein serving. The American Heart Association recommends that two servings of fish per week will help to keep your heart healthy. Fish is an excellent source of lean protein, and it is rich in omega-3 fatty acids, which have been known to aid in inflammation and decrease your risk of cardiovascular disease. Although fish does benefit the heart, a concern that arises with most people is the level of mercury found in fish. All fish may have traces of mercury in them. Most of the larger ones, like the older sharks, swordfish, and king mackerel, will have the highest levels, so if you are concerned about this, choose a fish which has less mercury, such as salmon, catfish, tuna, and shrimp. According to WebMD, for the most part, the level of absorbing mercury while eating fish is not a health concern; but, if you are pregnant or want to become pregnant, avoid the exposure. Adults can eliminate the mercury better than children can, so limit your children's exposure to mercury. As far as the fetus is concerned, there is a risk of damage to the brain and nervous system. There are better alternatives for obtaining omega-3 oils if you are concerned about the mercury or just do not like fish. Canola oil, flaxseed, walnuts, and pumpkin seeds are excellent sources of these fatty acids. If you do choose fish, not only can baking be a healthier cooking method, but deep-frying may also increase the concentration of mercury in your fish. To avoid mercury contamination, the American Heart Association suggests eating about six to seven ounces per serving but no more than twelve ounces per week. Those with heart disease and high triglycerides may require more fish than others, so be sure to speak with your doctor on the amount of fish that will benefit you the most.

So, with the discovery that only three to four ounces of meat is required on a daily basis, I am sure you are concerned about where to locate the remaining protein you need for your daily intake. As discussed earlier in this chapter, you can obtain protein from other sources, such as nuts, eggs, and even soy. You have also learned that you can get protein easily from your veggies. Although some of your vegetables may only contain one to two grams of protein, eating them together will quickly add up to your daily intake, and the nutritional benefits will be amazing—as we will discover in the next chapter. Take the time to know what you are eating and how much of it you are eating. By reducing your intake of meat and diligently increasing your protein intake through vegetables, the healing power and nourishment that you want and will receive will amaze you, and, through this, God will be glorified.

Have no interest in being a vegetarian or vegan, but want to decrease your meat intake? Maybe being a "flexitarian" would better suit your needs. You can be someone who mostly eats plant-based foods, with occasional meat intake. Your meat intake would be mostly poultry and fish, with limited red meat. Just be sure that vegetables and fruit cover half of your plate, with whole grains taking the next-largest space on your plate, and protein taking no more than one-quarter of your plate (which means about three to five ounces of protein).[23, 24]

---

[23] Mayo Clinic Staff, "It's Time to Try Meatless Meals, Mayo Clinic, July 26, 2017, https://www.mayoclinic.org/healthy-lifestyle/nutrition-and-healthy-eating/in-depth/meatless-meals/art-20048193.

[24] Lizzie Streit, MS, RDN, LD, "The Flexitarian Diet: A Detailed Beginner's Guide," Healthline.com, July 29, 2018, https://www.healthline.com/nutrition/flexitarian-diet-guide.

Chapter 4

Fruits and Vegetables

M Y GOAL FOR THIS chapter was to not be someone who
created another fruit-and-vegetable section that most
people would just skip over, because most people by now
know that eating more fruits and vegetables will give you the best
results of a healthier body. Nor did I want to just say, "Eat your fruit
and vegetables"; end of subject. I wanted to take you to a different
aspect of why these foods are essential and why they need to be the
biggest part of your daily intake. So, in this chapter, I want to introduce
to you two words that go hand in hand with fruit and vegetables—
acidic and *alkaline* (*basic*)—and the science behind them.

The measure of whether a solution is acidic or alkaline is known
as "pH" (potential of hydrogen). The scale for measuring pH is
from 0 to 14. For those of you who own fish, you may have a good
understanding of the pH levels and know that 7 is neutral; it is
neither acidic nor alkaline. Below 7 is acidic, and above 7 is alkaline.
You tend to learn this a little quicker when you have just killed your
daughter's goldfish and you were left to tend to them while they were

away with friends or on a trip. I know. Science class was reintroduced to me when I had to be the one to tell her I was the one who killed the fish. But bear with me as I take you down the road of Science 101 and my Basic Emergency Medical Technician Classes.

The term *acidosis* is an acidic pH in the body, which is caused by a diet of acid-forming foods, emotional stress, or any other process that deprives the cells of oxygen. The body will try to compensate by utilizing alkaline minerals. If your diet does not contain enough alkaline minerals, acidosis will occur, which results in impaired nutrient absorption and, eventually, weakened immune and detoxification systems. Acid buildup may impair cellular energy production, which could promote tumor cells and increase your chances for fatigue and illness. Additionally, a depletion of minerals can and will contribute to a long list of disorders, including but not limited to arthritis, osteoporosis, and neurological impairment.

Without much surprise and given the statistics of diseases that lie at the feet of this country, most if not all can conclude that our national diet may be too high in acid-producing animal products and too low in alkaline products, such as fruits and vegetables. So, what do these highly acidic foods tend to be? Mostly they are processed foods, sugars, white flour, beverages (coffee and soft drinks), eggs, dairy, and meats. Please do not think that I am going to try to convince you to be a vegetarian. I am not. But the best way to change your body to be a more alkaline body than an acidic one is to do one thing: change what you are eating.

Studies show that unless your body is slightly alkaline, it cannot heal itself. So, by choosing not to be aware of your pH levels, what you are consuming may not be effective in the healing process and you getting better. Without a proper pH level, your body struggles to absorb vitamins, minerals, food supplements, and other nutrients. The ideal blood pH is between 7.35 and 7.45, which is slightly alkaline. The stomach is usually at a pH of 3.4 so that it can break down food.

My blood results indicated my body was not absorbing vitamin D; therefore, I concluded my medication was not getting absorbed either. This meant I was more acidic than alkaline, and any medication they put me on was not helping. In order for my medication to help me, I had to change the food I ate, and I had to be aware of what that food was doing to my body.

A more alkaline body is where we all should begin in the process of healing and having optimal health. Educated choices of what you eat and the kind of nutrition you put into your body are key factors in how your body will react, or not react, to your medication and even your natural supplements.

Water is also a key ingredient. Hydration and eating a higher value of alkaline foods are the beginning basis of a pH balance that is optimal for your health and well-being. All this is according to www.coreonehealth.com/ph-in-the-balance. Also, according www. coreonehealth.com, a good rule of thumb is that your alkaline diet should be of 60 percent alkaline-forming foods and 40 percent acid-forming foods. You will also need to factor in how much of your total intake needs to be protein. Lemon in your water first thing in morning is a great way to start a hydration day. Even though lemons are acidic, they may be alkaline forming (a by-product when digested) in the body. Some studies indicate that, although there is no scientific proof, an excellent and inexpensive way to alkalize your water is by adding baking soda and coral calcium powder. This will not affect the pH levels in your blood, but it will help your urine become acidic, meaning your body is ridding itself of excess acids and your kidneys are functioning properly and doing their job.[25]

A high-acid pH level occurs from a high-acid diet. Your body naturally will try to compensate, but if your body is unable to adjust to these high levels a buildup of acid in the cells will begin. The result will cause a host of problems, such as leg cramps, premature aging, bladder problems, kidney stones, headache, hormone problems, muscle aches and cramps, dry skin, weight gain, osteoporosis, immune deficiency, low energy and chronic fatigue, stress, pale

---

[25] Alina Petre, MS, RA (CA), "Lemon Juice, Acidic or Alkaline, and Does it Matter?" Healthline.com, December 2, 2016, https://www.healthline.com/nutrition/lemon-juice-acidic-or-alkaline.

complexion, stomach ulcers, lower body temperature, yeast/fungal infections, gastritis, susceptibility to infections, free-radical damage, depression, thin nails, dull hair and split ends, skin irritation, and sensitive teeth.[26]

The list can go on. But I think you get the picture. As your read this book, do any of those symptoms fall on your lap? I know they did on mine. And I knew my body was more acidic than alkaline. To test your alkaline level, all you need is pH strips, which can be bought at a health store or an apothecary shop. Or, you can hold your breath; if you can't do that for more than twenty seconds your levels may be too high in acid. Again, human blood should have a slight alkaline range of 7.35–7.45. Below or above this range means signs and symptoms of illness and/or disease. Anything from 6.8 and below, and 7.8 and above, means the cells in your body will stop functioning, and your body will die. The extra buffering the body requires because of a high acidic level can make any person prone to chronic and degenerative diseases. This decreases the body's ability to produce energy, repair damaged cells, and detoxify itself, therefore making you more susceptible to lack of energy and prone to more illnesses. This important pH level is not just about what you eat; it's about how you think and feel as well.

The good news is that your body can turn to alkalosis just as quickly as it can turn to acidosis. It is a balancing act, and you need to eat from both sides; but, remember, it is very important to eat more from the alkaline side.

How interested in fruits and vegetables are you now? Do you want to know how to keep your pH level up (alkaline)? Vegetables, peas, beans, lentils, seeds, spices, herbs, and seasonings, along with nuts, help maintain a good pH level. Acid-forming foods include meats, fish, poultry, eggs, refined grains, sugars, some fruits, and, of course, processed foods.

---

[26] Elisha McFarland, "Signs Your Body Is Too Acidic & Here's What to Do to Correct It," Collective Evolution, August 29, 2017, https://www.collective-evolution.com/2015/09/10/signs-your-body-is-too-acidic-how-to-correct-it/.

Staying aware of your pH level can be of great advantage to your health. But there is no need to be obsessed with it. If you choose to keep an eye on it, you can test your levels through saliva or urine. Test in the morning and at night. If the test reads above 7.5, eat more acid-forming foods; if it is below 7.5, eat more alkaline-forming foods. The more you are aware of your pH balance, the less you may find yourself not testing it. But, if you choose this route, please note that an alkaline diet may not level out your pH results, especially if you already have a parasitic infection or inflammation. So be sure to stay in touch with your doctor on any health changes. Just being aware of your pH level can improve your health.

In the meantime, as I have encouraged you from the beginning of this book, do your own research. Read the article I found by Dranne M. Minich, PhD, FACN, CNS, and Jeffrey S. Bland, PhD, FACN, entitled "Acid-Alkaline Balance: Role in Chronic Disease and Detoxification."[27]

Food's Impact on the Body at the pH Level

Are the foods you eat acidic, alkaline, or both? Use the groupings below to help you learn how to categorize your food to increase awareness of your pH balance.[28]

Acidic Substances

The foods in this group increase acidity in the body, leading to acidosis. The number at the beginning of each list indicates the pH level of those foods.

---

[27] Dranne M. Minich, PhD, FACN, CNS, and Jeffrey S. Bland, PhD, FACN, "Acid-Alkaline Balance: Role in Chronic Disease and Detoxification," *Alternative Therapies* 13, no. 4 (Jul/Aug 2007).

[28] https://trans4mind.com/nutrition/AirWaterLife-FoodImpactOnBody-pH-Chart.pdf.

3.0: bacon, sausage, processed cheese, cola, pudding, french fries, other fried foods, canned tuna, lobster, ice cream, nuts and most roasted nuts, hazelnuts, sugar-added grapefruit and orange juices

4.0: most legumes, snow peas, tomato sauce, veal, buttermilk, cream cheese, granola, white bread, flour tortillas, artificial sweeteners, white vinegar

5.0: most frozen and canned vegetables, cooked swiss chard, navy beans, most wild game, cottage cheese, barley, oat bran, rice cakes, most wines, powdered or liquid stevia, balsamic vinegar, cigarettes, iodized table salt

5.5: pomegranates, garbanzo beans, lima beans, chicken, turkey, duck, goose, lamb, goat, venison, elk, processed cereals, white rice, semolina, wheat bran, white and wheat flour, brazil nuts, sesame oil, safflower oil, almond oil, reverse-osmosis filtered water, most bottled water and sports drinks, brown sugar, chocolate custard with white sugar, sweetened yogurt, tapioca, ketchup, mayonnaise, mustard, vanilla, and most pharmaceutical drugs

6.0: dates, figs, prunes, other dried fruits, cooked cranberries, black-eyed peas, peeled potatoes, most pickles, cooked zucchini, salmon, tuna, most other fish, oysters, most shellfish, plain yogurt, cornbread, tortillas, Cream of Wheat cereal, most whole-grain breads, popcorn with salt and butter, rye, wheat and wheat germ, pistachios, pine nuts, Kona coffee, soy milk, rice milk, almond milk, salted butter, pumpkin-seed and grapeseed Oils, processed maple syrup, sulfured molasses, gelatin, and hummus

6.5: green bananas, plums, cooked green peas, horseradish, kidney and pinto beans, pickled olives, cooked spinach, cooked whole eggs and egg whites, liver and other organ meats, processed milk (cow and goat), processed dairy products, most cheeses, oats, buckwheat, corn, and rice breads, cornmeal, buttered unsalted popcorn, sprout breads, sunflower seeds, wheat, rye, and Rice Crackers, whole grains, rice vinegar, soy cheese, soy sauce, carob, fructose, pastries made with honey and whole grains

Neutral Substances

The foods in this group are neither acidic nor alkaline, so their value is 7 (the middle of the pH scale).

7.0: eggs yolks (cooked soft), unsalted butter and margarine, raw milk (cow and goat), raw whey (cow and goat), brown and basmati Rice, municipal tap water, canola, corn and sunflower Oil, barley, malt syrup, raw honey

Alkaline Substances

The foods in this group increase alkalinity in the body, promoting alkalosis. The number at the beginning of each list indicates the pH level of those foods.

7.5: blueberries, fresh coconut, raw cranberries, fresh guava and sapote, strawberries, bamboo shoots, beets (without the greens), chives, cooked brussels sprouts and broccoli, cooked squash and eggplant, fresh corn, cooked kale, cooked soy beans, okra, potatoes (with skin), radishes, tofu, flaxseed, millet, spelt, quinoa, chestnuts, unprocessed apple cider, grain-based coffee substitutes, flax, avocado, and primrose oil, raw maple syrup, homemade mayonnaise, sea salt, tamari sauce

8.0: apples, currants, gooseberries, ripe bananas, fresh oranges and peaches, bell peppers, cauliflower, raw green cabbage, fresh mushrooms, jimaco and arrowroot, fresh pumpkin, fresh ripe olives, fresh tomato, turnip, parsnip, and kohlrabi, turnip greens, wild rice, sesame seeds, almonds, natural unsweetened fruit juices, sake, fish oil, unsulfured molasses, most fresh herbs and spices, miso soup, vegetable sea salt, apple cider vinegar

8.5: blackberries, cantaloupe, honeydew, most other melons, fresh apricots, fresh dates, fresh figs, grapefruit, grapes, kiwi, nectarines, fresh pears, papaya, passion fruit, raisins, alfalfa sprouts, sprouted grains, carrots, fresh garlic and ginger, ginseng, green beans, kudzu root, most lettuces, onions, leeks, rutabaga, taro root, fresh sweet peas, ginger and mu teas, cayenne, cinnamon

9.0: loganberries, persimmons, fresh mangos, pineapple, fresh raspberries, tangerines, artichokes, beets (with the greens), raw celery, raw cucumber, endive, raw eggplant, raw red cabbage, sweet potatoes and yams, dried soy beans, unfrosted dried pumpkin seeds, watercress, raw zucchini, green and herbal teas, cilantro, parsley, stevia plant, kelp, karemgo, seaweed, and other sea vegetables

9.5: watermelon, raw broccoli, straw, wheat, lemongrass and other green grasses, potato skins (not fried), raw kale, raw mustard greens, fresh raw vegetable juice, blended green-grass drinks

10.0: fresh lemon, raw brussels sprouts, raw swiss chard, kimchi and other fermented vegetables, raw spinach, baking soda

Now take a second look at this list. See anything familiar? Maybe you noticed some of the many fruits and vegetables that you have read about, heard of in the past, or remember learning were good for you. Some could very well even be cancer-fighting foods. You may recognize anything at the 7.0 level or above as very popular, healthy, and cancer-fighting foods; some may even be labeled as antioxidants. These foods put your body into healing mode at the cellular level. This chapter is not intended to get you to look into the pH diet. By no means is that what this is about. My intention is to offer knowledge that will help you make informed choices. A better understanding what your body is doing and how it reacts to the foods you eat may help you make better choices. The information in this chapter simply offers another view of what you eat, so you can see that all those processed foods, sugars, and meats are not on the good side of the pH scale and, therefore, should be eaten sparingly and wisely.

This different perspective on fruits and vegetables, and why they should be included in your diet in greater amounts than meat, bread, and sugar, should kind of make you want to say, "Oh wow!" That was my reaction. Not just because certain foods—or too much of them— were actually making me sick, even though I thought they were healthy to eat. It's amazing to see how strategically and thoughtfully God designed His plan. His attention to detail in everything is all so that we could eat to be at our optimal health. We only need to eat what He provides for us, and no more. He loves us that much. Look at the list and, just for kicks, really see what God provides for us to be healthy, as opposed to what is man-made (or processed) that is keeping us unhealthy. It is all there, and so are the choices that we make.

Meat was long considered expensive and even hard to find or be able to cook. Maybe, just maybe, there was an underlying reason why meat was only served on special occasions and why so many advocates encourage minimizing meat intake. At 150 pounds, your meat protein intake should only be 10 percent of your daily total food intake. Look at where meat is in the grouping of acid and alkaline foods. Meat is too acidic to eat it at every meal, every day; doing so hinders the healing process your body needs at a cellular level. Maybe now you understand why although meat may not bad for you, it is not good for you to eat as much of it as we in this society do on a daily basis. I say, do like they did in the past; save the meat for a special occasion, and find other sources of protein for your daily intake. I found it to be a very easy transition to only have meat protein on weekends, and, honestly, I didn't miss it. Eat your fruits and vegetables. Look, our bodies can be forgiving, and they can bounce back. For the most part, they will. And you can still take detours toward a diner, drive-in, or dive to indulge in your favorite foods—you just can't do it every day.

Chapter 5

Bread

B READ, IN THE SIMPLEST form, is nothing but flour, water, and salt; however, when yeast (or another leavening agent) is added, it rises to life and becomes a hugely popular food. Americans consume approximately fifty-three pounds of bread per person, per year—a little more than a pound per week. Bread is popular around the world and is one of the world's oldest foods. It is commonly prepared for any and all meals throughout the day, is often served as a snack or appetizer, and can even be prepared as a dessert. Although most bread doughs are baked, some can be steamed, boiled, cooked, or fried. The process of making bread, some thirty thousand years old, is a skill mastered by artisans around the world. And, as legend has it, whoever eats the last piece is supposed to kiss the cook.

Growing up, it seemed my mother constantly kept me on a diet. It amazes me now that weighing 120 pounds in my teens seemed less acceptable than weighing the same amount when in my thirties, although I was the same height. No matter my age, bread was taboo, my nemesis. This is true for most people struggling with their weight. In my forties, I feared bread not because of my weight but because of the gluten. So, it seemed that all my life bread had been my enemy. First, it was a product that made me fat, and then it became a product that could do me harm. Where was the happy medium? How could a product that had been around for so many years, a product that represents the body of Christ, become so damaging to someone's digestive system that it leaves him or her doubled over with pain and nausea? I could not imagine that I was supposed to live the rest of my life overwhelmed by multiple trips to the bathroom. I refused to succumb to this condition; I was not going to accept that this was just how things were going to be for me. All my life it seemed that bread had gotten the best of me, and now I was going to fight back.

When I first thought that I might be gluten intolerant, I actually imagined that eliminating gluten would be a quick fix. But it wasn't. I soon discovered how much food had gluten in it, and my quick stops at the grocery store ceased. I spent hours at the store reading labels, looking for a few items that I could eat. I pored over every label, every ingredient. There were times when I would put off going to the store because the misery of shopping literally brought tears to my eyes. Then, I found apps that could assist me in finding products that were safe for me to eat. That reduced my time somewhat, but I still found myself spending hours shopping.

Eating had truly put me in a depressive state of mind. I began to fear eating and constantly worried if what I was about to eat would be a trigger, whether the very moment I ate it or later, when I was on the road heading toward home. There were times when I ate out with a friend, and four bites into the meal, I had to run to the bathroom, where I spent the rest of the evening. *Embarrassing* is an understatement for describing those days.

Going out of town on a gluten-free diet was almost a total disaster. As the months went by, it seemed that gluten-free products were on the rise, much like the fat-free craze that went on years before. The labels were out there, and finding the products I needed became easier, but they weren't better. Some tasted okay, but others—well, there are no words to describe what they tasted like. The gluten-free bread was absolutely terrible. The whole loaf of bread felt like a brick, weighed about as much, and tasted like … I've never actually eaten a brick, but you get the idea. When people asked me about gluten-free food, wanting to know what it was, I always responded, "If you can say, 'Yum,' after your first bite, it probably has gluten in it." I found myself once again abstaining from bread, until my daughter talked to me about gluten intolerance and my situation. I then began doing more research and discovered that gluten might very well no longer be the enemy that we all have considered it to be.

Recent studies[29] show that one out of one hundred people suffer from intolerance to gluten; this places celiac as two times more common than the other ADs (Crohn's, ulcerative colitis, and cystic fibrosis, for instance) combined. Statistically, that means a total of about 3 million suffering with celiac in the United States. It is thought that these self-attacks and destructions are possibly caused by certain proteins, and since gluten is a protein, when ingested, it is believed that this is what causes the inflammatory immune system reaction. Research has discovered that in someone with this allergy (gluten intolerance), the villi in the small intestines become damaged, and what would normally be absorbed, such as vitamins and other nutrients, can no longer be absorbed. With the body having the inability to absorb the needed nutrients, you have the result of several diseases, mostly autoimmune, including thyroid disorders. Keep in mind that, since your body is not absorbing those nutrients, the medications you are prescribed to take are also not getting absorbed. I have had many arguments with my doctors because the lab results were showing I wasn't taking my medication, and I was. Each visit my prescription strength was increasing, and my absorption rate was lowering, but no one took notice. I had to double my pain pills when I was sick with swollen lymph nodes, because the pills were not working. These studies led me to have an aha moment.

---

[29] Gluten Intolerance School, glutenintoleranceschool.com.

Do you see any pattern here? A similarity in any of the chapters so far? Absorption as a result of intestinal damage is the pattern and problem that keeps repeating. This malabsorption is often called the "leaky gut syndrome."

So, you get the results, and gluten ends up being the bad guy, the one that has to go. Really? Is gluten all that bad, or, once again, have we re-created it to be bad, and, therefore, has become intolerable to our system?

Let's return to the science room for a spell. Gluten is a protein, a protein that is found in wheat, barley and rye: three grains that have been around since God created the plants on the earth.[30] To find the gluten you have to break down these grains. In a grain's natural state, the whole grain is comprised of the entire seed. The seed is made up of three edible parts: the bran, the germ, and the endosperm. The bran is the outer skin of the seed, which contains antioxidants, B vitamins, and fiber. The germ is the part of the plant that has the potential to sprout into a new plant; it also contains important nutrients like B vitamins, protein, minerals, and healthy fats. The third layer is the endosperm, the "outer layer," which is the food source for the embryo and the largest portion of the seed. This endosperm contains starchy carbohydrates, proteins, and small amounts of vitamins and minerals. When you process the grain, the bran and the germ are normally removed, leaving only the endosperm. Without the endosperm and bran, 25 percent of the protein is lost, and seventeen nutrients are lost as well. What is left is the endosperm's gluten and starch. This is a part of the grain they don't even feed the cows, because it will kill them; it is nutrient dead. You can't expect to split up a team and expect good results.

This was a grain that once, as a whole entity, had 90 percent of the vitamins and minerals and proteins you would ever need.[31] Once it is milled into flour, it will begin a kind of dying process, and

---

[30] Sue Becker, "A Kernel of Truth," Bread Beckers, July 16, 2010, https://www.breadbeckers.com/blog/kernel-of-truth/.

[31] Sue Becker, "Do Not Eat the Bread of Idleness, Bread Beckers, 1994, https://www.breadbeckers.com/blog/bread-of-idleness/.

within three days, the flour is old. Vitamins have to be added back into the product, which gives you the "enriched" flour that you buy at your local grocery store. But not all the vitamins and minerals can be replaced, and you can never get back the fiber and protein that were lost when the grain was processed by removing the two most important components and then enriching it. Although some of the vitamins are added back, possible pesticides, preservatives, and bleaching products (such as chlorine) are also added into the product during the processing of the food. These are the results you get because commercially processed food needs a shelf life, so the grain had to suffer—and in the end, we suffer too. Since this product has to have vitamins replaced, does that in itself tell you how much of the health benefits have been lost to begin with?

Our bodies are designed to process food by breaking them down in order to use the nutrients. The body secretes certain enzymes from the pancreas, the liver, and some by the small-intestinal wall; these enzymes—amylase, protease, and lipase—are used to break down carbohydrates, proteins, and fats to the point where they can be absorbed through the cells lining in the small intestines. The only substance that then needs to be further processed by the body is protein, which the body must break down into amino acids. The enzymes above are found in the hull (outer layer) of the grain, and they are the essential enzymes needed for this process and for the body to break down gluten. They are the key factor for enabling the absorption of essential nutrients by the body.

Not only are we a nation of meat eaters, we are also a nation of processed foods. Foods that have become so readily available that our bodies no longer have the ability to digest food as it was actually intended to be digested, including breaking down the foods we were intended to consume: whole foods. These whole foods include the consumption of all the layers of the grain, including the outer layer of the seed. This part of the seed contains most critical nutrients that are the primary factor for optimal digestion and nutrition. Your body needs these enzymes to begin the process of digestion, and when your body no longer gets those enzymes, it loses the ability to break down the food. What is left as undigested in your system, your body does not like, so it begins to reject it by creating an allergic reaction to get rid of it. The results are an upset stomach, cramps, nausea, and frequent urges to use the restroom—all of which leads to damaged intestines. This is where the gluten intolerance comes in, because the important enzymes needed to break down the gluten protein are not there. Why? Because they have been removed. I also feel that because we eat so much processed food and so little whole and natural food, the villi in the small intestines become dormant and damaged from the lack of the digestion process; therefore, absorption of these nutrients is inhibited, and then ADs begin to emerge.

Think of the muscular system. If you do not use the muscles in your body on a daily basis, eventually, they lose the ability to function. I feel this is the same concept with the digestive system. If the digestive tract does not function as it was actually intended to, it loses that ability. Exercise can rebuild muscle, and muscle is said to have memory as well. I believe we can rebuild the digestive system too, and then it will regain its full capacity to function the way it should and as it was intended. Just like the muscular system, I think the digestive system has memory, and it can and will remember its innate ability to break down the protein it needs, and to do so in the manner in which it was intended. The process begins with each and every one of us. It begins with eliminating the processed breads, and the bleached and enriched flours, including anything that does not provide whole grain in your diet. This is the first step to getting you on your way to a healthier you, and it brings back the body God created to work in the way He intended it to work.

Gluten is not the enemy. How the grain is processed, and how the much-needed nutrients are lost in the process, is the combined cause and the root of the problem. Below are statistics from the USDA[32] that will allow you to see for yourself the nutrients found in whole grains versus the nutrients lost in processed flour:

[32] The Bread Beckers, Inc., USDA Handbook no. 456.

Nutrient	Hard Red Wheat Flour	Whole-Wheat Flour	White Flour (Unenriched)	White Flour (Enriched)
Calories	1,497	1,656	1,651	1,651
Protein (g)	55.8	54.4	47.6	47.6
Fat (g)	8.2	5.9	4.5	4.5
Carbs (g)	325.2	336.1	345.2	345.2
Calcium (mg)	209	109	73	73
Phosphorus (mg) 1,606	866	395	395	
Iron (mg)	15.4	5.9	3.6	13*
Potassium (mg)	1,678	431	431	431
Thiamine (mg)	2.35	1.16	0.28	2*
Riboflavin (mg)	0.53	0.33	0.21	1.2*
Niacin (mg)	19.5	9.3	4.1	16*

* Based upon the minimum required levels of enrichment

This is just a compressed, short list; remember, more than twenty-five nutrients that are found in whole grains are lost in the process of creating white flour. Many diseases manifest themselves from vitamin and nutrient deficiencies, including but not limited to MS, ADD, fibromyalgia, PMS, IBS and IBD, dementia, and even depression. The bran is full of fiber, which helps in absorbing nutrients and removing toxins as it scrubs the digestive tract. Just adding bran will eliminate one pill most Americans take: dietary fiber supplements. These are illness that could be eliminated or possibly reversed just by eating freshly milled real whole-wheat bread. This bread still may not be for everyone, though; there have actually been cases of some people with gluten intolerance (about 1 percent) who may still have a negative reaction. Be aware it may not help everyone the way it helped me.

When it comes to eating properly and dieting, this real bread is something you should not fear. In fact, you should be ecstatic when eating it. These grains are low in fat, they provide energy for the body, and they are high in protein. The high fiber aids in the reduction of obesity and manages diabetes. Placing these whole grains into your daily diet can reduce the risk of heart disease, lower your cholesterol, and reduce the risk of some cancers, such as colon and breast cancer.

My results: I am back to eating bread, every day. I no longer have the fear of having gluten intolerance, because my body is now accepting the gluten in the manner that it was supposed to be digested—whole. My stomach no longer cramps under the pressure of gluten rejection, and bowel movements are on more normal and manageable terms: every day without fail, and sometimes twice a day. This is something I know most women suffer with, even without the other complications of IBD. I also no longer have the fear of bread making me fat, because I know that, in moderation, whole grain gives me the nutrients I need to aid in optimal metabolism—something I lacked for nearly fifteen years. Oh, and it taste great! I am a firm believer that, once you begin to eat freshly milled whole-grain bread, you will not eat anything else. I found this out when my daughter and I went to my favorite restaurant specializing in gluten-free cooking. It was the worst hamburger I ever ate. It tasted actually stale. The bread I cook is fresher, has more flavor, and even feels fresher and lighter than store-bought bread. Although it can be a bit time consuming, this bread is in my home always.

So, how do you begin the process of milling your own grains? First, you need to find a grain mill. Start with a search on the internet, and do your research. Look at the reviews from those who have purchased the mills. You may even find that your food processor has an attachment that you can purchase. They range in size and price. I wanted the optimal milling process, so I looked for stone grain mills. Although they can be expensive, maybe a group of your neighbors could go in together to purchase one and share it. This is what my daughter and I did until I found the one I liked. In the long run, you will be saving money when you no longer have to purchase the processed breads—not to mention the medical expenses. Next, you need to find a local company or an internet company that sells the grains whole. Typically, these grains are sold in airtight buckets. You then keep the grain in the bucket until you are ready to mill the grain.

You only mill the amount of grain that you will use that same day. Remember, once the grained is milled, the process of losing those essential nutrients will begin: 40 percent within the first twenty-four hours; after seventy-two hours, the product will turn rancid. It does not mean you can't use it. It just means most of the good nutrients are gone. That flour will make really good sourdough bread, though, so it won't go to waste. I keep the excess and use it for dusting the flour board if I didn't mill enough. Placing it in the refrigerator can extend its life as well. The longer you mill your grain, the more you will know exactly how much grain it will take to make your bread. Don't be afraid to experiment and try new recipes. These milled grains work beautifully in the bread machine as well. Yes, milling and making your own bread can take time and maybe some trial and error. For me, it was a lot of trial and error. The freshness will last about a week, maybe two weeks—more than processed bread. There will not be any waste, and you have nothing but great-tasting, healthy, unprocessed, and nonchemical goodness. For that, you will definitely thank God and glorify Him for what He has given.

Chapter 6

Good Oils/Bad Fats

T HIS CHAPTER I FEARED. Almost to the point that I thought
it would not be necessary to include it in my book. All the
information on oils was already out there, so there would be
no need to bore you with information about saturated and unsaturated
fats. My theory was that this chapter would merely be a filler and
nothing else, but God had other plans. Once again, I would feel his
instructions powerfully, letting me know that I was not to deviate
from His plan. I was shopping in a local grocery store for my usual
list of fruits and salads and the other ideal, minimally processed foods
that I wanted to have for the week, and I came across a book on the
shelf. Right then and there I had my second aha moment.

For about six years now, I have been trying to convince people
that there is a certain oil that is far better for you than any other oil,
including olive oil. My research on this oil was shockingly surprising.
No one wanted to hear about it. Although they would sit down and
listen to me, despite my efforts to convince them otherwise, the words
"saturated fat" still freaked them out. Everyone was willing to try

it when I sautéed spinach with it. But no one was willing to take it further and consume it every day, much less with every meal, as I do. This book would be tool to finally convince others, and it was God's way of letting me know I was on the right track and this chapter will be just as important as the others and shall not be omitted.

Most Christians quite often agree that there are times in life when a split second goes by, and you immediately know that God is speaking to you and showing you the right path to take. I was standing there in the store, holding in my hand the book I just mentioned seeing on the shelf, and at the very moment of reading just the words on the front cover, I knew God was still working with me on *my* book. I could feel His presence come over me. I remembered God's words to Peter: "Do not call anything impure that God has made clean" (Acts 10:9). These words began to repeat themselves in my head again and again.

I knew in that instant that I had been on the right track all along, and I had to get the word out to everyone about how wonderful this product that comes from what the Bible may refer to as the palm tree. It is another food that has been given a bad rap, just like gluten.

The Coconut and Coconut Oil

It was not shocking to me when I discovered that the coconut palm is sometimes referred to as the "Tree of Life" in the Philippines; Spanish explorers called it *coco*, meaning, "monkey face," because the three indentions (or "eyes") on the hairy nut looked like the face of a monkey.[33] Although this is a nutritious source of meat, juice, milk, and oil that has fed and nourished populations around the world for generations, it was labeled a food that was not good for us in the 1960s.[34] Quite notably, this was the same time as the introduction

---

[33] Wikipedia, Coconut, https://en.wikipedia.org/wiki/Coconut.

[34] Alex Rinehart, "Why Coconut Oil Made Its Remarkable Comeback," Articles, April 10, 2016, https://info.dralexrinehart.com/articles/nutrition-benefits/why-coconut-oil-made-its-remarkable-comeback.

of the soybean and its oil. Coconut is undergoing a new discovery and now is being recognized as highly nutritious, rich in fiber, vitamins, and minerals. It is classified as a "functional food" because it provides many health benefits beyond its nutritional content, and its healing properties go far beyond those of any other dietary oil, according to the Coconut Research Center and Dr. Bruce Fife, CN, ND, author of *The Coconut Oil Miracle*.

To understand the difference between coconut oil and other oils, you must understand how each oil is classified. Oils are composed of molecules called fatty acids. There are two methods of classifying fatty acids. One is based on their saturations; there are saturated, monounsaturated, and polyunsaturated fats. These are the classifications that most people use to base their decisions on purchase and use of products when reading the saturations on the labels of the products that contain oils in them. The second is based on the length of the carbon chain within the fatty acid. Each fatty acid is classified as a long-chain fatty acid (LCFA), a medium-chain fatty acid (MCFA), or a short-chain fatty acid (SCFA). Each chain is metabolized differently, according to the length or size of the chain. The longer the chain, the more likely your liver will store the fat for use as energy at a later time. The shorter the chain, the quicker your liver will release the fats for immediate energy use.[35]

Most fats and oils, whether saturated or unsaturated, whether from animals or plants, are comprised of the long-chain fatty acids. This means that nearly most, if not all, of your daily intake of fat is made up of these long-chain fatty acids. These are the fats that can build up in your arteries, causing your cholesterol levels to increase. Coconut oil is composed of mostly medium-chain fatty acids, which are commonly known as medium-chain triglycerides (MCTs). Therefore, it does not have a destructive effect or lead to elevated cholesterol, and it actually helps to prevent heart disease and reduce

---

[35] Mary Janes Brown, PhD, RD (UK), "MCT Oil 101—A Review of Medium-Chain Triglycerides," Healthline.com, May 21, 2016, https://www.healthline.com/nutrition/mct-oil-101.

the risks of atherosclerosis.[36] The best source of these medium-chain fatty acids is coconut and coconut-palm kernel oil.

I am not going to stop here. The reduction of heart disease is a good start (do your research, as some doctors still think differently, and this may be more hype than truly healthy),[37] but what if I told you that most, if not all, of the unsaturated oils that are purchased in the store, processed and refined—primarily vegetable oils—are already rancid by the time they even reach your favorite grocery store?[38] These oils are heated, bleached, and deodorized, which requires heating these products up to about four hundred degrees Fahrenheit. This heat creates oxidation, which forms free radicals that can have negatively affects to your health. Even the cold-pressed or expeller-pressed unsaturated oils will negatively affect your health once heat is added to them, creating oxidation and the formation of free radicals. Proper usage, packaging, and storage must be strict to prevent oxidation and the formation of these free radicals.

In 1950, Denham Harmon (February 14, 1916–November 25, 2014) created a "free radical theory of aging," which basically stated that organisms age because cells accumulate free-radical damage over time. Free radicals are a by-product of normal cell function. When cells create energy, they also produce unstable oxygen molecules. These molecules, called free radicals, have a free electron. This electron makes the molecule highly unstable. The free radical bonds to other molecules in the body, causing proteins and other essential molecules to not function as they should. Initially, his theory was limited to aging, but, in later years, he expanded his theory to include

36   Larry Canale, "MCT Oil Benefits: How Medium-Chain Triglycerides Can Bolster Our Health," University Health News, June 25, 2018, https://universityhealthnews.com/daily/nutrition/mct-oil-benefits-medium-chain-triglycerides-may-help-heart-brain-weight-control/.

37   Robert H. Shmerling, MD, "Coconut Oil: Heart-Healthy or Just Hype?" Harvard Health, April 13, 2018, accessed October 21, 2018, https://www.health.harvard.edu/heart-disease-overview/coconut-oil-heart-healthy-or-just-hype.

38   HealthyLiving, https://healthyliving.azcentral.com/what-are-the-dangers-of-rancid-oil-12533524.html.

age-related diseases when he discovered a link between free-radical damage and a range of disorders, such as cancer, arthritis, Alzheimer's disease, diabetes, and atherosclerosis, according to Wikipedia.[39, 40]

Saturated fats are not susceptible to oxidation or to the formation of free radicals. You will find that some foods will have these saturated fats added to them to prevent the spoilage caused by free radicals. These fats can be exposed to heat, light, and oxygen without a huge degree of concern for oxidation and free-radical formation. For this reason, saturated fats are a preferred source to use for heating and cooking foods, and, especially, for storing foods. The higher the saturated fat, the less likely that you will have the negative effects from heating the oils. Coconut oil, as a highly saturated fat, becomes the best and safest source for cooking oil, and it is a natural preservative for storing foods as well. When cooking with coconut oil, your food will not become greasy, unlike the other oils you are used to cooking with. When frying with coconut oil, you will be able to tell the difference. Yes, *frying*. … You can even deep-fry with coconut oil just by keeping your heat setting between 325 and 375 degrees Fahrenheit. Deep-fry anything you want; but keep in mind that just because you deep-fry an Oreo cookie in coconut oil, although it maybe tastier, it still will not make this snack a healthy one. (Just sayin'!)

When you feel that your life has been turned upside down, to the point where you have to first know the locations of all bathrooms no matter where you are, and your condition is controlling, you will go to any measure to research what it will take to get your life back to the "normalcy" of before. At least that's what I did. You will also try anything and hope it works. I did that too. Just like millions of others, nothing worked for me. No matter what I did, every day, there was fatigue, low blood pressure to the verge of passing out, diarrhea, cramping and aching, along with the fear of food. With that came more prescribed pills and concoctions. Finally, I said,

---

[39]   Wikipedia, https://en.wikipedia.org/wiki/Denham_Harman.

[40]   Denham Harman, "Aging: A Theory Based on Free Radical and Radiation Chemistry," *Journal of Gerontology* 11, 3 (1 July 1956: 298–300), https://doi.org/10.1093/geronj/11.3.298.

"Enough!" No one should have to live like this. This was not what God intended. God's plan will always include that He wants us to be healthy and strong so that we can carry out His "working plans" with strength and sure focus. I knew this, without a doubt. But how to get there became very frustrating. So, as I look back to years ago and see myself researching night and day to find the answers, I now have come to realize that I did not find the coconut; the coconut actually found me.

It was an accident that I stumbled onto a website that provided the scientific structure of this amazing fruit. Or was it? I recall my pastor saying every once in a while, "God does not create junk, and He doesn't have accidents." Back then, there was very little information to go on, except the fact that it was easily digested, and your body used it immediately for energy. That was all I knew. I cooked with it, sautéed spinach, and although it was very yummy, that was really it. It wasn't until later, as I was writing this book, that I discovered the coconut is truly making a comeback, and people are really listening. So, through more reading and research, I replaced my everyday oils, lotions, and deodorant—and many other things— with coconut and coconut oil. Remember the lady in the Franks Red Hot Sauce commercial and what she always said? Well, welcome to my relationship with the coconut, because I do the same thing. Yes, I put that awesome stuff on everything. I fry with it, I drink it, I bake it in my bread instead of using other oils, and I even use it as a moisturizer after I shower. I have even replaced my deodorant with coconut oil. Some people even brush their teeth with it. I have! It has helped reduce the sensitivity of my teeth, and it can reduce plaque and possibly help with gum disease. Three tablespoons a day is an amount known to even help people to lose weight. As an additive, I use coconut water in my smoothies first thing every morning. The coconut improves digestion and aids in nutrient absorption.[41] When I am sick, I drink one tablespoon of coconut oil with a glass of orange juice, three times a day, to help knock out that ugly common cold.

---

[41] SunWarrior, https://sunwarrior.com/healthhub/the-healing-wonders-of-coconuts.

Before you put socks on, a little coconut oil rubbed on your feet will control both sweat and odor. The results: no stinky feet, and they become the softest feet you have ever felt. I wash my hair every three to four days. Before shampoo, I condition my hair for at least twenty minutes with, yes, coconut oil, which can also minimize dry scalp and dandruff.[42] My results have all been successful and satisfying. I feel better now that I am using an all-natural product on my body, eliminating the unwanted chemicals that are put in deodorants, conditioners, and other products. This means fewer complications and less absorption of unwanted chemicals in my body. Coconut is no longer just for that Easter Bunny cake that your mom makes every year (like my mom does). It's for life—every day of your life. So, whether you're in a grocery store or on a tropical beach, pick up a coconut and examine it. Consider the many wonders and possibilities contained within—the medicinal properties, yes, and even something deliciously fun, like a fresh coconut cake. Coconuts may not be as pretty or as colorful as, say, the blueberry or pineapple, but when you remove that hairy outer shell, this wonderful fruit can impact millions of lives, including yours.

Coconut oil is packaged in two ways: refined or unrefined. The difference is the processing. Refined is taken to an extra stage by removing particles and other unwanted substances. This extra stage allows for a higher heat to be used when cooking, and that one-of-a-kind coconut smell is removed because the refining process deodorizes the oils. It is also tasteless. Unrefined, also called pure coconut oil or virgin coconut oil, is unfiltered and without any additives. Naturally, it is also more nutritious because it is unprocessed and has not been subjected to heat, as the refined has. Of course, because of supply and demand, the refined may be cheaper and possibly more available. But I have never come across a day at the grocery store where I could not find either. Some may state that the unrefined is best suited to be used only externally, whereas the refined is best suited

---

[42] OrganicFacts, https://www.organicfacts.net/health-benefits/oils/health-benefits-of-coconut-oil.html.

for consumption. These choices tend to be left up to the consumer. Do your own further research to decide. I keep both kinds in my house. The refined is better suited to the kitchen, whereas I keep the unrefined in the bathrooms and bedroom. This is for two reasons: (1) I happen to love the smell of coconut, and (2) I find the unrefined does rub on the skin more smoothly than the refined. You will find it does not take much for this beauty oil to cover your body. But I will warn you: beware of your dogs; they love it! Bynx (my greyhound) just loves the stuff, so when I brush my teeth, he waits patiently for a treat of it. It is a great little snack for your furry four-legged friends. And when I am not looking, he will find his way, trying to get into the container. Trust me, they will eat it till it is all gone. Bynx did. I had to fight Merlin (my daughter's Morkie a Maltese-Yorkshire mix) from trying to lick it off my legs when I applied it after my shower.

If what I have already told you still has not convinced you to give coconut oil a try, consider just this one thing: what I reported earlier in this chapter about unsaturated fats and the negative impacts of heating them, plus the discussion that most oils purchased in the grocery store are already rancid (often before they even arrive at the store) because of the heat used during the processing of those oils.[43] Some of these oils have already been heated to four hundred degrees, causing the oxidation process to begin even before they are put on a truck to be delivered. Manufacturers may refine and deodorize the oil to mask the detection of it being rancid. Consuming rancid oils is not good for you. It increases your cholesterol, causes more weight gain, contributes to diabetes and other ADs, and promotes aging.[44] Before you pick up another bottle of unsaturated oil, research it yourself. Do you not want to use the freshest, most natural product to feed your family? You buy the freshest vegetables, fruits, breads, and meats. Why wouldn't you do the same with your oils and make sure they are just as fresh and as healthy? You owe it to your and your family's

[43] HealthyLiving, https://healthyliving.azcentral.com/what-are-the-dangers-of-rancid-oil-12533524.html.
[44] LiveStrong, https://www.livestrong.com/article/459786-can-you-get-sick-from-eating-rancid-oil/.

health to make the right choices and to know exactly what you are putting into your body.

An update in 2017 showed that coconut oil is again starting to get a bad rap. NBC News reported on it as a "Health Hero or Dietary Disaster."[45] USA Today also reported, "Coconut Oil Is Out."[46]

In July 2016, *Organic Spa Magazine* released this statement:

> At one point hydrogenated and vegetable oil manufacturers started demonizing coconut oil because of its high saturated fat content (coconut is about 60 percent fat with just over 94 percent of this saturated). These claims have now been widely disproven. Coconut oil is an extremely healthy saturated fat. Its principle fatty acid is lauric acid (also found in human breast milk), a medium chain saturated fatty acid or triglyceride (MCT) that has potent antiviral, antifungal, antipathogenic, and antimicrobial properties. Lauric acid powerfully strengthens the immune system. It optimizes our body's absorption of vitamins, minerals, and amino acids, enhancing overall health. It can help assuage digestion-related problems, such as heartburn and irritable bowel syndrome. Why, it's even used to treat AIDS and candida because of its antipathogenic effect in the gut. In vitro, it's been shown to inactivate the HIV, measles, and herpes simplex viruses, among others. Coconut oil's healthy fat has also been proven to promote heart health, maintain normal cholesterol levels, stimulate metabolism, improve thyroid function, and give a mighty boost to energy levels–which combined can help in decreasing body fat, while increasing muscle. The benefits of organic

[45] NBCNews.com, https://www.nbcnews.com/better/wellness/should-you-really-be-putting-coconut-oil-everything-n748526.

[46] WebMD, https://www.webmd.com/diet/features/coconut-oil-and-health#1.

coconut oil, and in particular, its lauric acid/MCT content, simply cannot be overstated.

In June 2017, J. J. Virgin, celebrity nutrition, fitness, and mind-set expert, and contributor to *Huffington Post,* stepped up to the plate and debunked the "hotly debated" report released by the American Heart Association advising against the use of coconut oil, blaming the high level of saturated fat and "no known offsetting favorable effects"[47] as being "inaccurate and outdated." Virgin further states, "The American Heart Association relied on 50-year-old studies to state their case, The doubts that have surfaced about coconut oil are a great reminder of why it's key to have current, fact-based information from trustworthy sources."[48]

I have noticed over time that there will always, for the most part, be controversy about almost anything. What works for one, may not work for others. But knowing how it works and how it could possibly benefit you is a start in the right direction. Mayla calls the palm tree *pokok seribu guna* ("the tree of a thousand uses").[49] So, what do you think it can do for you? Or, better yet, what do you think it *can't* do?

[47] http://circ.ahajournals.org/content/early/2017/06/15/CIR.000000000 0000510.

[48] Huffington Post, https://www.huffingtonpost.com/entry/yes-coconut-oil-is-still-healthy-its-always-been_us_5950b5bee4b0326c0a8d09ad.

[49] Kelly Jadon, "The Coconut Palm: A Tree of Life," *Digital Journal: A Global Digital Media Network,* December 20, 2013, http://www.digitaljournal.com/life/food/the-coconut-palm-a-tree-of-life/article/364322.

Chapter 7

Sugar

A S I DID MY research on this subject, I found that God
had given me an even tougher challenge: finding all the
information I could to base a true, unbiased conclusion
as to everything related to sugar. There was so much information, I
could not have truly gone through it all without hiring a multitude
of researchers. Again, I found myself in over my head and relying on
God to help me. I found it so difficult to sift through all the good, the
bad and the ugly. I had to stay in line with what this book was truly
intended to be about; starting always from the beginning. With that
in mind, I discovered some amazing information and a result that
led to some astonishing findings.

Again, with no surprise, I was able to find some scripture referring
not to sugar itself but to sugarcane or "sweet cane." But you have to
still look deeper into history and what sugarcane was truly intended
for. But it seemed the only place where I could find scripture that
mentioned sugarcane was Isaiah 43:24 and Ezekiel 27:19. Later, I
would discover two other mentions of "sweet cane," both in the

book of Joshua, possibly referring to the location of the sugarcane by the River Kanah, bordering the land of Asher. Sugarcane is native to India, and the time line of sugar will come a little later in this chapter. But I encourage you to read Dr. Schar's article on sugar, sugarcane, and the history of sugar; you can find this article on his website.[50] What I discovered through Dr. Schar and other resources is that sugar is not only a highly marketable product, but the juice in its natural form is also a highly nutrient-dense food.

So, what is sugarcane juice? In order to answer that question, first, you have to take the scientific route to discover what sugarcane juice *is not*. It is not a simple sugar, and it does not contain any simple sugar.

Simple sugars are carbohydrates, which are found in many different foods. There are both simple carbohydrates and complex carbohydrates. Both are utilized in the body for energy, but one is much better for you than the other. A simple carbohydrate only stays in your system long enough to be stored as fat. It is a contributing factor for diabetes and weight gain, and it also can have an unhealthy impact on the fluctuating level of blood sugar for both diabetics and nondiabetics. This fluctuation is also known as a sugar spike. Complex carbohydrates stay in the body longer and typically provide more nutrient value for us to obtain those fibers, proteins, vitamins, and minerals that are needed to sustain a much healthier lifestyle. Since cane juice is not a simple sugar, it is a friendly compound for diabetics, without having the side effects that simple sugars provide, which can be a compacting factor to their health. A simple sugar includes sucrose (table sugar), glucose, fructose, and galactose. These simple carbohydrates are what you mostly find in processed foods. Sugarcane juice *is* sugar, but it is sugar in its raw, natural form.

Removing the molasses and color from the sugarcane sets the stage for the refining process, which ultimately provides the end result of the white crystals known as table sugar (sucrose). Raw sugar can

---

[50] DoctorShar.com, www.doctorschar.com/archives/sugarcane-sacharum-office inarum/.

be consumed in its natural state; refining it removes any unwanted taste and impurities and takes away any nonsugar ingredients, which, I think, includes removing valuable nutrients in the process.[51] To get to the best state of the sugar, the part that benefits you, you need to understand the value sugarcane had before processing, during which it was mixed with water, crushed, boiled, spun, and separated, with chemicals added, including lime, phosphoric acid, and diatomaceous earth.[52] The juice is rich in fiber (thirteen grams) and antioxidants; it is not empty calories, and it can also play an important role in hydration.

Naturally, raw sugar is good and good for you. It has the nutrients and minerals needed to sustain a healthy lifestyle. Sugar has a very important role to play in regard to our health. Our brain has a necessity for sugar. Without it, we can't function mentally or physically. The body will become diaphoretic (sweaty); you will lose consciousness, become incontinent, and have difficulty breathing. If left without sugar long enough, death can occur. The nutrients found in sugarcane are beneficial to the functioning of internal organs, including the kidneys, heart, brain, and sexual organs. Studies have shown that, because of its alkaline nature, sugar can be effective in fighting cancer cells, such as in the breast and prostate.[53] Surprisingly, as I mentioned earlier, sugar is also known to help with rehydration, not only cooling the body but also energizing it with a high quantity of useful carbohydrates and proteins. Sugar contains phosphorus, calcium, iron, magnesium, and potassium. With all this to gain from natural raw sugar, why would you give it up to have processed table sugar?

What happened? Why did we begin to break down and process the sugarcane? More money? More power? I may not be able to answer that question in full, but I think we can all agree that there

---

[51]   ImperialSugar.com, https://www.imperialsugar.com/sugar-101/How-Sugar-is-Processed.

[52]   MotherEarthNews.com, https://www.motherearthnews.com/real-food/sugar-facts-myths-zmaz71sozgoe.

[53]   nutrition.indobase.com/articles/sugarcane-juice-nutrition.php.

was money in sugar, and so sugar meant money. There are some indications that the Indians have been producing sugar for four thousand years. In 327 BC, sugarcane was discovered in India by an officer in the army of Alexander the Great.[54], [55] It had to be intriguing and satisfying to the palate. I am sure he thought, *Everyone is going to love this.* This "honey powder" was named *khanda,* which became what we call candy. Could it be that the wheels inside their heads were turning? No, not yet the embrace of sugar in Europe, which came much later. In AD 350, the Indians discovered how to crystallize sugar by boiling it, and this was when refining began. In the 400s, honey was still the number-one sweetener in India, despite Indian ability to produce larger quantities of sugar. Between AD 500 and 600, China was introduced to sugar, and plantations of sugarcane were created. This was also when the first descriptions of sugar in the urine and its occurrence in obese individuals would be mentioned.

By 1095, the trading of sugar, commonly called "white gold," began. In 1200, the Egyptians wanted in, and they would become the masters of sugar. By 1319, a kilo of sugar was valued at two shillings per pound. Today, that is about eighty-eight dollars, leaving it as a commodity only for the rich and noble of that time. In 1493, sugar was brought to the New World by Christopher Columbus during his second trip. By 1500, Central America had started establishing its own sugarcane plantations. In Europe, the Renaissance had already begun. By 1600, beets were used for the purpose of extracting their sugar.

By this time, more than one hundred reports had been written specifically about diabetes or at least mentioning it as a health concern. In 1674, Thomas Willis, an English physician, expanded the term diabetes, calling it *diabetes mellitus,* because of the "sweetness of the urine." (*Mellitus* means "honeyed" or "sweet" in Latin.) By the eighteenth century, sugar was a product starting to no longer be expensive, making it ever more accessible to more and more people

[54]   http://www.sugarhistory.net/who-made-sugar/sugar-timeline/.
[55]   http://www.timerime.com/en/timeline/1352177/Sugar+Changed+the+world/.

and, therefore, more and more popular. The average consumption of sugar at that time was about four pounds per year, per person. Rheumatoid arthritis (RA) was discovered during that era by a french medical student. By 1900, the average amount of sugar consumed was about forty pounds per year, per person. In 2005, it jumped to nearly one hundred pounds per year, per person (just under ten tablespoons per day).

With every action there is a reaction. It took almost eight hundred years for sugar to spin its web and create the beginning of our autoimmune epidemic. Was sugar the actual push for these ADs, including diabetes? Diabetes was around before sugarcane was "discovered" and processed. But was type 2 diabetes around?

Just as there is a reaction for every action, there is also a recourse for every course. Sometimes, it is best to leave things just the way God had intended—left alone to be pure and clean. Sugar was so pure, so perfect.

The sugar age ended before 1750, since there were new discoveries to pull sugar from the beet. Then, there was the discovery of high-fructose corn syrup. Fructose and a few artificial sweeteners were created, which just became ways to cut costs and increase the production of processed foods. So, these cost-effective products actually become a by-product that negatively affects our health. In 2008, the obesity rate of Americans was at 33.7 percent, and diabetes had increased to 24 million.[56] For the first time, in 2015, the Dietary Guidelines Advisory Committee advised consumers to "cut back" on the amount of added sugars in their diet by half.[57] You think? The latest survey showed an increase to 39.6 percent for the year 2016.

Your brain can use at least 120 grams of glucose per day to function, according to Mark Sisson of *Mark's Daily Apple*.[58] Glucose is a form of sugar your body naturally creates from the carbohydrates

---

[56] https://stateofobesity.org/obesity-rates-trends-overview/.

[57] https://hippocratesinst.org/the-sugar-timeline.

[58] Mark Sisson, "How Much Glucose Does the Brain Really Need?" *Mark's Daily Apple*, June 19, 2014, https://www.marksdailyapple.com/how-much-glucose-does-your-brain-really-need/.

you eat. This glucose is created by the liver. Once it is created and enters the bloodstream, the muscles and organs utilize it as energy. Here is where fruit can play a huge part in the process. Fruit will get into the body at a steady rate as it is digested in the stomach. The complex carbohydrates work in the same manner as the fruit. This gives you energy for hours without the "crashing" effect of refined sugars. Refined sugars and the brain do not work this well together. (This is what God knew when He created humans.) Remember, these are the sugars in cookies, cakes, breads, desserts, and other processed foods. At first, you get the "sugar high" as your brain secretes serotonin. This makes you happy. The massive increase in the blood sugar signals the pancreas to start pumping out large amounts of insulin. Once the insulin gets into the bloodstream, it soaks up the sugar to store for later use. This deprives the brain, the muscles, and the other organs of energy. This is the "sugar crash." You are tired, weak, and unable to focus. Together, the sugar high and the sugar crash cause you to crave more sugar. The reaction: a sugar binge and, soon to follow, the high risk of obesity and diabetes. This all could be prevented by using sugar in its rawest form. The bottom line is simple: nutrients and consuming in moderation both were lost in the process of refining sugar. Maybe we should have stuck to just eating honey.

Sugar and Those Substitutes

Sugar comes in two different forms: dry (fine, coarse, and sanding) and liquid. All forms have their very own flavors, and some will be sweeter than others. Each and every one may be distinct in origin, but, according to some studies, once your body has broken down the sugar (to glucose), it will all be used in the same way: for energy. But be aware that glucose is the sugar vital to your life, not fructose.[59] Although your body may not know if the sugar came from a fruit,

---

[59] Healthline.com, https://www.healthline.com/nutrition/why-is-fructose-bad-for-you#section1.

vegetable, or a processed food (created by humans), sugars can and will be metabolized very differently.

The dry sugars consist of the granulated, super-fine white sugars, whereas the coarse and sanding sugars are classified as brown sugars with rawer content, such as coconut sugar, turbinado, demerara, raw, malt, and maple sugars. Claims have been made that these sugars have more trace minerals and nutrients as a result of minimal processing. The liquid sugars are syrups, such as maple, honey, and molasses. Most of the sugar content and calories per gram remain the same for each. On average, each gram of these sugars contains about four calories per teaspoon, and all are low-glycemic when used in moderation. When comparing potassium in micrograms per 100 grams in some of the sugars, coconut has the highest of 1,030 milligrams, maple has 234 milligrams, and refined sugar comes in last place with 2.5 milligrams. For a less-processed alternative with a small amount of nutrients, try to find Sucanat (an abbreviation for *Sucre de canne naturel*, meaning "natural cane sugar"), which is dehydrated sugarcane juice. You will find it has trace amounts of iron, calcium, vitamin B_6, and potassium, unlike the refined sugar that loses these nutrients during the processing.

Artificial sweeteners, although approved by the FDA for home use, have the characteristics of being anywhere from 160 to 700 times sweeter than regular sugar. Although some may be synthetic or natural, they are still classified as high-intensity sweeteners.[60] Even though they have been effective in weight loss and help those suffering with diabetes to regulate their sugar levels, it may be a better alternative to just avoid refined sugars and eat the less-processed foods to reduce your sugar intake.

Reducing your sugar intake and kicking the sugar craving and habit can be done in several ways. Eliminating your intake of sugary soft drinks and candy sets off an instant decrease, quite remarkably, along with reducing your caloric intake. Spending less time in the

---

[60] https://www.health.harvard.edu/blog/artificial-sweeteners-sugar-free-but-at-what-cost-201207165030.

center of the grocery store and more time along the perimeter will also allow you to make healthier choices of fruits and vegetables. Most items in the center of the store are products of processed and sugar-added foods. Paying particular attention to the sugar content prior to purchase will eliminate consuming more sugar and avoiding excessive intake. This will allow you to make your snacks at home and provide healthier choices at mealtime. Eating more whole fruits, vegetables, and proteins will decrease those sugar cravings, increase the longevity of your energy, and simultaneously decrease the side effects of sugar spikes and crashes.

The value of substituting molasses for sugar in baking comes from the generous levels of minerals present in molasses that are absent from sugar, as mentioned earlier in this chapter. Molasses provides high levels of calcium, copper, and iron and can be a great help if you are suffering from anemia. In addition, the level of sugar is lower in molasses, so, if you're interested in reducing sugar intake, molasses can act as a low-sugar substitute.

Finally, be aware of what you are eating and make wiser choices when you do go out to eat. Have your dressing on the side so that you are in control of your portions, and ask for nutrient content so that you are aware of the sugar. If time permits, look up the menu online before you go, so you spend less time poring over the menu at the restaurant and more quality time with the people you are with. Get motivated and set your goals for two days with less processed sugar, then four, and so on (baby steps). Each day will get easier. You may not always notice the difference, but your body will.

If you just feel that you *must* have the refined sugar—your sweet tooth just can't have it any other way—moderation is the key you need. Remember, no matter the form of sugar, the content of sugar is the same, so moderation is the key, whether the sugar is in its raw state or a processed form. Try to maintain a lifestyle without refined sugar, limiting yourself to a special treat once a week or once a month. Better yet, cook and bake with raw sugars, and you will find the only change is within your health. When making bread, I personally stick with honey or molasses, depending on the bread I am baking.

I was helping out a friend and teaching him better ways to have a healthier lifestyle, and I introduced him to coconut sugar. He was leery of the change but gave it a try. He took it to his work and put it in his coffee. He was amazed at the difference. He said he had always thought that his "jitters" were from the coffee, even though he normally only drank one cup per day. It turned out his jitters were from the refined sugar, and he never had white sugar in his coffee again. It is amazing how small changes can and do make a big difference.

As I conclude this chapter, I will not fail to mention the dangers of the other sugars. Artificial sweeteners and sugar substitutes, although they may be derived from sugar, are not at all the same as sugar. Even if they say they are all natural, they are still processed and refined, including agave nectar. Even though you may think you are reducing calories, these little pink and yellow packets are not the way to go for a healthier lifestyle; in fact, they can be more damaging to your health than being overweight. Some studies have suggested that using artificial sweeteners could make you hungrier and still raise your blood sugar, despite the fact that fructose was designed to have a lower glycemic index and to minimize those unwanted sugar spikes. I think it was mainly designed to be cost effective and cheaper to produce when processing foods for the consumer. But the worst is yet to come. The side effects and health risks associated with these artificial sweeteners are actually scary: enlarged livers, skin rashes, diarrhea, headache, bladder issues, stomach pain, and even cancer, according to some studies.[61] Even if there is validity to or confirmation of these accusations, is it worth the risk of trying to find out? Bottom line, I say, if God didn't make it, don't use it. If you want an alternative, more-natural sweetener, turn to honey, molasses, date sugar, organic maple syrup, and maybe even coconut sugar. Stay with minimally processed sugars and read the labels. Do your own research. It is important to know what you are putting into your body, how it can affect you today, and what the results will be if you continue consuming it in the days, months, or years to come.

---

[61] https://drpeterosborne.com/artificial-sweeteners-toxic-side-effects/.

Chapter 8

The Essentials of Vitamins, Minerals, and Metals

ETHANOL, BENZENE, AMMONIA, FORMALDEHYDE, hydrochloric acid, petroleum esters and derivatives, cyanide, coal tar, acetone, cattle brains, sulfuric acid. Like me, you may recognize some of these chemicals and substances as ingredients listed in many of your household products, for cleaning and such. You also may have no clue what these chemicals and substances are. Believe it or not, these are just some of the ingredients you may find in your vitamins. Most vitamins in supplement form are processed with a petroleum derivative or hydrogens sugars.[62]

Methanol is also known as methyl alcohol. Although it is produced naturally, it is a chemical used as an antifreeze. Benzene is also an

---

[62] http://www.doctorsresearch.com/articles4.html.

73

organic chemical compound, but it is a compound of crude oil and an important component of gasoline. Acetone is the common product used as a nail-polish remover. I am sure you are fully aware of the chemicals formaldehyde and cyanide. All this time you were thinking you were just taking your vitamins, but, instead, along with all those vitamins and minerals A through Z, you have been ingesting all these other chemicals and substances. These chemicals and substances are used to produce the synthetic versions of what God has already provided for us in the fruits, vegetables, and meats that He created for us to eat.

The best way to get your vitamins is, of course, through eating whole foods. If supplementing, there are two ways to obtain vitamins: nonfood vitamins or real-food vitamins. Most vitamins sold are not real-food vitamins; they are synthetically made supplements processed with petroleum and/or hydrogenated sugar extracts—even if you see "natural" on the label(s).[63] They do not even have the same chemical or structural forms as the real vitamins found in food; therefore, will not be natural in the human body, according to "The Truth About Vitamins in Nutritional Supplements."[64] Only foods or supplements composed of 100 percent real foods can be relied upon as not containing nonfood vitamin analogues (i.e., chemicals and other substances used in synthetic processing). Even if the label indicates "vegetarian formula," it does not mean the product is healthier or that chemicals and other substances have not been used to produce the product. It just means animal products have not been used in the processing. There may still be extracts from the chemicals listed at the beginning of this chapter, including but not limited to formaldehyde, other acids, and industrial chemicals. Even though most of us are taught that there is no difference between nonfood

---

[63] http://www.doctorsresearch.com/articles4.html.

[64] Robert Thiel, PhD, Naturopath, "Doctors' Research Nutrition from Food, What a Concept!"; "The Truth about Vitamins in Nutritional Supplements" (blog posts), dates unknown, https://www.doctorsresearch.com/articles4. html.

and real-food vitamins, I urge you to read the labels. You would be shocked to discover what you are truly putting into your body.

Through studies and research, it has been discovered that the human body does break down the nonfood vitamin differently. For instance, vitamin E, when used in the synthetic form, is actually recognized as toxic by the liver, and the body accordingly tries to rid itself of the vitamin as quickly as possible. The liver has a specific transport for the vitamin, which is found only in food and not in the synthetic form of the vitamin. And let's not forget the fact that vitamin E found in food is 2.7 times better than that of the synthetic when it comes to the body's ability to retain the nutrient.

When it comes to utilizing the vitamins in real food, the benefits can range from 10 to even 100 percent more effective than that of any vitamin produced in a pill form. An article from "Natural Whole Food Vitamins," in the website www. thedoctorwithin.com, states it best:[65]

> Vitamins are not individual molecular compounds. Vitamins are biological complexes. They are multistep biochemical interactions whose action is dependent upon a number of variables within the biological terrain. Vitamin activity only takes place when all conditions are met within that environment, and when all co-factors and components of the entire vitamin complex are present and working together. Vitamin activity is even more than the sum of all those parts; it also involves timing. Vitamins cannot be isolated from their complexes and still perform their specific life functions within the cells. When isolated into artificial commercial forms, like ascorbic acid, these purified synthetics act as drugs in the body.

---

[65] http://www.doctorsresearch.com/articles4.html.

They are no longer vitamins, and to call them such is inaccurate.[66]

Ascorbic acid, commonly known as vitamin C, is not vitamin C. There are certain components in naturally occurring vitamin C (i.e., in foods) that allow for oxidative-damage repair. Oxidative damage occurs in your cells from a buildup in reactive oxygen species (ROS), such as metabolism, as well as the interactions with toxic sources from cancer-promoting substances and drugs, including radiation.[67] Normally, our body and its cells can and will defend themselves against ROS, preventing the damage by the use of free radicals and antioxidants. Without this, there is an increased risk of arthritis, heart disease, aging, GI disorders, MS, cancer, and neurological diseases. It takes a negative oxidative reductive potential, which is found in whole foods containing vitamin C, for the repair of the oxidative damage that has occurred.[68] Ascorbic acid has a positive oxidative reductive potential; therefore, it cannot replace vitamin C, or provide the total benefits of vitamin C, no matter how much you take.[69]

The foregoing examples are just a few instances representing how each and every one of us has been deceived into thinking that these vitamins and other products are truly good for us, when, actually, they are not. Companies pay big money to promulgate this information in order to maintain high profits from low-cost supposedly nutritional products that are anything but that. We have become a fast-food, pill-popping society. We are too busy and way too hungry to take the

[66] Tim O'Shea, DC, "Ascorbic Acid Is Not Vitamin C—Whole Food Vitamins: ★ The Doctor Within," The Doctor Within, June 15, 2018, http://thedoctorwithin.com/Ascorbic-Acid-Is-Not-Vitamin-C.

[67] NCI Dictionary of Cancer Terms, National Cancer Institute, https://www.cancer.gov/publications/dictionaries/cancer-terms/def/reactive-oxygen-species.

[68] Doni Wilson, MD, Chris Greene, Doug Kruckner, Ross Tyrrell, Dolly, Susan, Aman, Meg, Donna, B. Zeaux, Russell, Elvie, and Sheila K Liewald LAc, "5 Signs of Oxidative Stress and 7 Ways You Can Stop It," Doctor Doni, October 2, 2014. https://doctordoni.com/2014/10/5-signs-of-oxidative-stress/.

[69] Robert Thiel, PhD, Naturopath, "The Truth About Vitamins in Nutritional Supplements," http://www.doctorsresearch.com/articles4.html.

time to eat properly, and it is easier to just take a pill to ease the pain or satisfy the deficiencies in our bodies. Our bodies deserve much better than what we give them. The human body is far too complex and precious for us not to give it everything it needs and everything God intended it to have. We rarely settle for second best in our way of living. Why settle for second best in what we put in our bodies?

Genesis 1:29 tells us: "And God said, 'Behold I have given you every herb bearing seed which is upon the face of all the earth, and every tree, in the which is the fruit of a tree yielding seed; to you it shall be for meat.'" Genesis 9:3 tells us that God said, "Every moving thing that liveth shall be meat for you; even as the green herb I have given you all things." In both of these verses and throughout the Bible, I have yet to find any instructions where God said, "Oh yeah, don't forget to take your vitamins." Why? Because God didn't forget our vitamins. He created the human body; He knows what it is made of, how it works, and what it needs to maintain a healthy lifestyle. He didn't have to instruct Adam or Eve—or anyone else, for that matter—to take their vitamins, because those vitamins were already in everything God has already provided for us. Everything we need to sustain life is already in the fruit, the vegetables, and the meat.

Approximately 68 percent of Americans take some form of supplements to obtain their vitamins. We do not have the confidence that we are getting sufficient nutrients in our food today. Processing food is a transformation of raw ingredients into food for consumption, or of food into other forms. It typically takes clean, harvested crops or butchered animal products and uses them to produce attractive, marketable food products, often with a long shelf life. To some extent, this process dates back well into prior centuries, but modern food processing wasn't developed until the nineteenth and twentieth centuries.[70] This commercial processing of food was, in large part, designed to serve military needs. It was meant to remove toxins and

---

[70] Shruti Sethi, MD, "Principles of Food Processing," Horticulture Post Harvest Technology, NSDL, September 10, 2007, http://nsdl.niscair.res.in/jspui/bitstream/123456789/410/2/Revised%20principles%20of%20processing.pdf.

preserve foods, which resulted in enabling marketing and distribution. It alleviated food shortages and was intended to improve the overall nutrition of populations, as it made many new foods available to the masses. But, at the same time, this affects the nutritional value of food, since a lot of nutrients are lost in this process. Vitamin C is lost in the heating process, for instance. On average, any given nutrient is has lost 5 to 20 percent of its value by the time it reaches store shelves—a number that might not seem significant, but in its highest form would vastly improve the total overall quality of life and health. With the processing of food also comes high sugar (processed and imitation) content, which leads to diabetes. Lower-quality fats are used, resulting in higher cholesterol levels and more cardiovascular diseases, as well as the many ADs discussed throughout this book. All this should be reason enough to encourage us to opt for whole, unprocessed foods—only that which was intended and specifically designed for our bodies by God.

Here is another disturbing fact. A study conducted back in 2009 discovered that only an approximate 32.5 percent of Americans ate two or more fruits per day, and only 26.3 percent ate three or more vegetables per day.[71] That is less than the study in 2000, which showed 34.4 percent ate fruits, and 26.7 percent ate vegetables. In a nutshell, close to 75 percent of Americans eat in an unhealthy manner.[72] That percentage is a big number, and now we can clearly understand why ours is considered an obese society when compared to other countries. I suppose that this 75 percent reflects those individuals who provide the mass-market success and profitability of the medical and supplement industries producing these so-called vitamins and other miracle pills. If we could just reduce this number by half, and

[71] "Morbidity and Mortality Weekly Report (MMWR)," Centers for Disease Control and Prevention, September 10, 2010, https://www.cdc.gov/mmwr/preview/mmwrhtml/mm5935a1.htm?s_cid=mm5935a1_w.

[72] Bill Hendrick, "Americans Skimp on Fruits and Vegetables," MedicineNet, September 9, 2010, https://www.medicinenet.com/script/main/art.asp?articlekey=119554, reviewed by Laura J. Martin, MD.

get more people to eat better, those numbers, quite remarkably, would be reversed.

Vitamins

There are thirteen vitamins necessary to the human body: vitamins A, C, D, E, and K, plus the eight B vitamins (thiamine [B_1], riboflavin [B_2], niacin [B_3], pantothenic acid [B_5], pyroxidine [B_6], folic acid/folate [B_9], B_{12}, and biotin). All thirteen vitamins are essential for normal growth and development, from the moment of conception up to the moment of death. These vitamins are essential to maintain the health we need to help process the proteins, carbohydrates, and fats required just for us to breathe. All thirteen vitamins are readily available in whole foods, for each and every one of us, whether in what we grow in the garden in the backyard or purchase at the local grocery store. It should not really frighten you too much whether what you buy is organic or not. A lot of the vegetables and fruits could very well still be produced organically, but the cost and process to obtain the claim of "organic" on the label can be prohibitive. Many companies would rather forgo the claim and maintain a lower price for the consumer.

So, where are these essential vitamins, and which foods contain them? Below is a simple list of the thirteen essential vitamins and which foods contain them:

> **Vitamin A:** carrots, apricots, guava, papaya, broccoli, kale, mustard greens, spinach, swiss chard, winter and butternut squash, raw whole milk, and pumpkin—to name a few

> **Vitamin C:** apricots, avocados, blueberries, guava, papaya, red currants, broccoli, carrots, garlic, ginger, kale, mustard greens, spinach, most citrus fruits

Vitamin D: fish, ham, eggs, mushrooms

Vitamin E: sunflower seeds, almonds, pine nuts, peanuts, spinach, basil, oregano

Vitamin K: brussels sprouts, dark leafy greens, asparagus, cabbage, cucumber, onions, scallions, parsley, most herbs (dried and fresh)

Vitamin B$_1$ (Thiamine): sunflower seeds, pork chops, fish, pine nuts, pistachio, fish, pecans, macadamia nuts, most dried herbs and spices

Vitamin B$_2$ (Riboflavin): peppers, almonds, cheese, wheat bran, fish, sesame seeds, sun-dried tomatoes, most dried herbs and spices

Vitamin B$_3$ (Niacin): wheat bran, tuna, liver, peanuts, chicken, veal, bacon, sun-dried tomatoes

Vitamin B$_5$ (Pantothenic Acid): wheat bran, sunflower seeds, mushrooms, cheese, sun-dried tomatoes, fish, avocados, broccoli, squash, eggs, corn

Vitamin B$_6$ (Pyroxidine): wheat bran, pistachios, fish, sunflower seeds, sesame seeds, pork, hazelnuts, molasses (syrup), spinach, potatoes, peas, broccoli, asparagus, bell peppers, yams, garlic, most dried herbs and spices

Vitamin B$_9$ (Folic Acid/Folate): dark leafy greens, bean sprouts, beans, asparagus, peanuts, citrus fruits

Vitamin B$_{12}$: beef, lamb, eggs, cheese, turkey, pork

Biotin: swiss chard, carrots, almonds, eggs, strawberries, raspberries, halibut, cucumbers, cauliflower

Minerals

This section is a summary of the information I found on eMedicineHealth.com, in an article entitled "Minerals: Their Function and Sources." To learn more, check out their website. I found it very helpful.

The body needs many minerals, which are called essential minerals. Essential minerals are sometimes divided up into major minerals (macrominerals) and trace minerals (microminerals). These two groups of minerals are equally important, but trace minerals are needed in smaller amounts than major minerals. The amounts needed in the body are not an indication of their importance.

A balanced diet usually provides all of the essential minerals. The information below lists major and trace minerals, what they do in the body (their functions), and their sources in food.

Major Minerals (Macrominerals)

Sodium

Functions: needed for proper fluid balance, nerve transmission, and muscle contraction

Sources: table salt, soy sauce; large amounts in processed foods; small amounts in milk, breads, vegetables, and unprocessed meats

Chloride

Functions: needed for proper fluid balance, stomach acid

Sources: table salt, soy sauce; large amounts in processed foods; small amounts in milk, meats, breads, and vegetables

Potassium

Functions: needed for proper fluid balance, nerve transmission, and muscle contraction

Sources: meats, milk, fresh fruits and vegetables, whole grains, legumes

Calcium

Functions: important for healthy bones and teeth; helps muscles relax and contract; important in nerve functioning, blood clotting, blood pressure regulation, immune system health

Sources: milk and milk products; canned fish with bones (salmon, sardines); fortified tofu and fortified soy milk; dark leafy greens (broccoli, mustard greens); legumes

Phosphorus

Functions: important for healthy bones and teeth; found in every cell; part of the system that maintains acid-alkaline balance

Sources: meat, fish, poultry, eggs, milk, processed foods (including carbonated soft drinks)

Magnesium

Functions: found in bones; needed for making protein, muscle contraction, nerve transmission, immune system health

Sources: nuts and seeds, legumes, dark leafy greens, seafood, chocolate, artichokes, "hard" drinking water

Sulfur

Functions: found in protein molecules

Sources: occurs in foods as part of protein (meats, poultry, fish, eggs, milk, legumes, nuts)

Trace Minerals (Microminerals)

As mentioned above, the body needs trace minerals in very small amounts, but they are still essential to health. Even though iron is considered to be a trace mineral, the amount needed is somewhat more than for other microminerals.

Iron

Functions: part of a molecule (hemoglobin) found in red blood cells that carries oxygen in the body; needed for energy metabolism

Sources: organ meats, red meats, poultry; fish and shellfish (especially clams); egg yolks; legumes; dried fruits; dark leafy greens; iron-enriched breads and cereals; fortified cereals

Zinc

Functions: part of many enzymes; needed for making protein and genetic material; has a function in taste perception, wound healing, normal fetal development, production of sperm, normal growth and sexual maturation, immune system health

Sources: meats, fish, poultry, leavened whole grains, vegetables

Iodine

Functions: found in thyroid hormone, which helps regulate growth, development, and metabolism (I believe iodine contributed to my weight loss and health.)

Sources: seafood; foods grown in iodine-rich soil; iodized salt; bread; dairy products

Selenium

Functions: an antioxidant; it may also help with thyroid function

Sources: meats, seafood, grains

Copper

Functions: part of many enzymes; needed for iron metabolism
Sources: legumes, nuts, and seeds (chia); whole grains; organ meats; drinking water

Manganese

Functions: part of many enzymes
Sources: widespread in foods, especially plant foods

Fluoride

Functions: involved in formation of bones and teeth; helps prevent tooth decay
Sources: drinking water (either fluoridated or naturally containing fluoride), fish, most teas

Chromium

Functions: works closely with insulin to regulate blood sugar (glucose) levels
Sources: unrefined foods—especially liver, brewer's yeast, whole grains, nuts, cheeses

Molybdenum

Functions: part of some enzymes
Sources: legumes; breads and grains; dark leafy greens; leafy green vegetables; milk; liver
Other trace minerals known to be essential in tiny amounts include nickel, silicon, vanadium, and cobalt.

Colloidal Metals

Toward the end of my research I stumbled across a new amazing product. Although copper is listed as a trace mineral, I noticed that silver was not on this list. Silver is not a trace mineral. It is not an essential vitamin or mineral in terms of body balance or proper diet. It is simply a healing aid. Sure, I know this book is intended for healing the inside and eating properly, as well making sure your body stays balanced with the proper vitamins, but the outside is just as important, so I wanted to introduce you to what I discovered about silver and its benefits.

I came across the healing properties of silver while reading *Natural Cures "They" Don't Want You to Know About*, by Kevin Trudeau. The book led me to his website, www.naturalcures.com. This book and website helped me to get to another level in my research and improve my health, hopefully reversing my Hashimoto's disease. If you get a chance, I urge you to do two things: read this book and go to this website. Silver is, bottom line, a natural antibiotic. It kills all bacteria on contact. Like all antibiotics, it cannot distinguish between the good and the bad bacteria, so it will be necessary to take a probiotic if you choose to ingest the silver. I use the silver in a soap (for my hair and body/face [acne was reduced]) and in my toothpaste. (Six to eight sprays of it on your toothpaste or in your mouthwash will get rid of gingivitis and remove plaque [my dental hygienist spends less time removing plaque since I've been brushing with silver], and your dentist will tell you your teeth look great; mine did!) Silver can also be used as an antifungal to prevent and remove toenail fungus. Pour an ounce or so of silver in your own liquid hand soap, and you will have your very own antibacterial soap, and it really works. Bynx, my greyhound, had a chronic ear infection ever since retiring from the tracks. I cleaned his ears every day, but nothing cleared up the infection. Two drops of silver in his ears, and it was gone—and it has yet to come back.

For the Science Buffs

According to a 1996 report written by Richard Davies and Samuel Etris of the Silver Institute, there are three primary ways that colloidal silver can help heal the body:[73], [74]

1. **Catalytic Oxidation:** Silver naturally holds on to oxygen molecules, which readily react with the sulfhydryl (SH) groups that surround bacteria and viruses. In turn, this helps block the life-preserving cellular process known as cellular respiration, which is defined as "the set of metabolic reactions and processes that take place in the cells of organisms to convert biochemical energy from nutrients into adenosine triphosphate (ATP), and then release waste products."

2. **Reaction with Bacterial Cell Membranes:** Silver ions can attach to bacteria cell membranes directly and produce the same respiration-blocking effect.

3. **Binding with DNA:** Shown to literally enter bacterial DNA, up to 12 percent of silver has been detected in pseudomonas aeruginosa. (This is a bacterial infection mostly seen in postoperative patients, especially those on breathing machines. It can be a fatal infection that can cause death within twenty-four hours of contracting it. It has also been known to have great resistance toward pharmaceutical antibiotics.) According to one source, "While it remains unclear exactly how the silver binds to the DNA without destroying the hydrogen bonds holding the lattice together, it nevertheless prevents the DNA from unwinding, an essential step for cellular replication to occur."

---

[73] Richard L. Davies, and Samuel F Etris, "Colloidal Silver Facts," "The Development and Functions of Silver in Water Purification and Disease Control," 1996, http://www.csfacts.com/pages/davies.html.

[74] Ken Adachi, "Educate Yourself," "Silver Water (Colloidal Silver) Frequently Asked Questions," date unknown, https://educate-yourself.org/cs/csfaq.shtml.

Silver was used widely before the 1940s to aid in healing and preventing infections. It was even used in sutures. As medicine progressed, other, possibly better, products were developed for treatment and aiding the healing process. But in the 1990s, silver started making a comeback. Although there is a lot of information on the World Wide Web, research is still greatly needed for this product. It is not intended to be ingested for long periods of time (too much will make you sick), and, in some circumstances, it can interfere with medications you are currently taking. So, use caution, talk with your doctor, and, once again, do a lot a research and find out if the use of colloidal silver could be good for you. Personally, I love just using it as a cleansing agent in the shower. As mentioned, silver makes for a great soap.

Colloidal copper—well, the jury is still out. I find that it is unnecessary, since I get a good allowance of copper from the chia seeds that I put in my smoothies. Why buy something you already naturally get in your food? But I do spray the colloidal copper on my face as a refreshing mist; it helps reduce the fine lines and wrinkles, giving me a younger look.

Colloidal gold is supposed to support mental focus and concentration and improve eye/hand coordination. It is also thought to improve memory and promote a general feeling of well-being. Once again, do your research. Speak with your doctors on all these colloidal metals. I know that by just eating a healthy and well-balanced diet, I have improved my mental focus and concentration, and, in general, I feel great.

In summary, if you have to look outside your food to get the proper balance of nutrients, it seems to me that you are making it too complex, and then maintaining proper nutrition becomes complicated. The bottom line is simple: God has provided us with everything we need to maintain our bodies, sustain our well-being, and live long, healthy lives. Why would you alter anything, that has already been perfected for you?

Chapter 9

Portions, Sizes, and Servings

My flesh and my heart faileth: but God is the strength
of my heart, and my portion forever.

Psalm 73:26

WHEN IT BECAME CLEAR to me that I could actually reverse my situation into a healthier condition of no more worries, no more pain, and no more having to rush to find a bathroom, I knew I had to make several changes in my life. These changes would not just involve a new style of eating but a completely new lifestyle. It would have to involve a whole new concept of living, a new attitude, a different outlook on life, a reexamination of the way I treated myself and others. To effect these changes, I sat down and evaluated each area of my life that had an impact on my health and the way I lived, being honest enough to try to see how others might view my life. My pastor once said in a sermon on Sunday, "The way you live reflects the way you think." That statement did not touch me nearly as much then as it does now. In order to evaluate, I placed everything in its own section of my life, along with an action related to each and every one, with importance and need and then those desires. It is human to want to have all three, but my health could not be put on the back burner until all my other issues were dealt with. I had to face them all at once and on a daily basis work on each one, just like creating a new habit or breaking an old one.

There was so much that I wanted for my life—success with something new, peace and tranquility, and meaning. I wanted my life to be meaningful; when the time came, I wanted my obituary to be truthful. When people pass away, no one ever has anything bad to say about the deceased. Everyone always speaks of how good that person was, never having an ill word toward anyone, always happy, always willing to do good toward others, the list goes on and on. But I've often wondered how truthful an obituary can really be. Is it possible to make an obituary be true to life? So, I thought that if I wrote my own obituary while I was still alive and then adhered to those words, I could then evaluate and live my life to its fullest capacity, truly impact other lives for the better, and be the true witness that I needed and wanted to be.

Here is the obituary I wrote:

Tamera Shearon, age forty-six, passes away into the Lord's arms, rising to live with Jesus

She is survived by her three daughters and their husbands and one granddaughter. She is also survived by her mother and father, and a sister and brother. She was a mother of three, whose daughters will always remain in Christ's guidance because of the love she showed them and the love she had for Jesus. Despite the struggles and setbacks, she taught her girls to always maintain their glory and praise to the

Lord Almighty and never deviate from that, no matter
what was placed on their path. She was a firefighter
for seventeen years, serving the community of Fulton
County, Georgia, never complaining about the
service she provided and always smiling with every
task that was placed in front of her. She worked hard
by working two jobs to provide for her children. No
matter how tough it might be or how little money she
had, she always made sure her family had what they
needed, and she sacrificed her own needs to provide
for them. She was dependable, faithful, always there,
and never looking for anything in return.

Tamera's church was important to her and she
maintained attendance and served in many ministries
for the church whenever she had an opened
opportunity to serve. She always wanted and was
willing to do more, and her heart at times was heavy
because she couldn't. She never missed a church
service and honored God by walking in faith with her
tithes and offerings, and she trusted the Lord would
provide and bestow blessings upon her. She walked
with Christ every day on this earth; she did not leave
behind an unforgiven soul or a person who was not
touched or witnessed to. She ministered to all people
she came in contact with, either by her own works of
letting her light shine or taking the time to reach out
to any or all. Her voice was never raised in anger, and
she never passed judgment on anyone less or more
fortunate than she herself. God was always first with
her, and she was never moved from that, for He was
the One she feared. Her work was truly done, and now
God has her. Soon we will be with her, so let's now
celebrate her life here on earth, rejoicing that she, too,
lives and is with Christ her King.

After I wrote it, I was amazed that, at this very moment, this was not my life. I also admit that this is not the way most obituaries are written. But maybe these are the things you would like people to say about you when you have passed away, and writing it helps you reflect on the things you need to work on now, before it is too late.

In 1864, there was an explosion in a shed where people prepared nitroglycerin. Five people were killed, including a brother of the person you are about to read about. Determined to improve on the stability of nitroglycerin and to prevent this from happening again, dynamite was invented. Fast-forwarding to 1888, the death of his other brother is found in the obituary, but there is a mistake. He is actually reading his own obituary, which is entitled "The Merchant of Death." Because he profited from the sales of arms, the obituary stated that he "[the Merchant of Death] became rich by finding ways to kill more people faster than ever before, died yesterday." His disappointment with what he read, they say, was what motivated him to leave a better legacy. In 1895, he signed a last will and testament creating a widely regarded and most prestigious award available for outstanding contributions to humanity in literature, medicine, physics, peace, and chemistry contributions. He allocated 94 percent of his assets to establish the five awards. The first award would not be presented until 1901, as the Nobel Prize established by Alfred Nobel, five years after his death.[75]

On September 10, 1946, she left the convent and traveled by train to do what she described as "a call within a call" and took care of the poor while living among the poor. In 1950, she created an organization that would, in her words, "care for the hungry, the naked, the homeless, the crippled, the blind, the lepers, all those people who feel unwanted, unloved, uncared for throughout society, people that have become a burden to the society and are shunned by everyone." She started out with just thirteen people, and, by 1997,

---

[75]   Sean Braswell, "The Newspaper Error that Sparked the Nobel Prize," ozy.com, October 9, 2015, https://www.ozy.com/flashback/the-newspaper-error-that -sparked-the-nobel-prize/40007.

it had grown to four thousand nuns managing orphanages, AIDS hospices, and charity centers worldwide, caring for refugees, the blind, the disabled, the aged, alcoholics, the poor and the homeless, and victims of floods, epidemics, and famine.[76] In 1979, she, too, would give her acceptance speech when receiving the Nobel Peace Prize. Before her death September 5, 1997, Mother Teresa's Missionaries of Charity was operating 610 missions in 123 countries. Her secret to her success, she always said, was simply this: "I prayed."

Actually writing your own obituary may be a great tool to help you analyze your life and how you want to affect others in terms of your desired legacy. It is an important tool that gives you the control to be true to yourself and to others. With a plan, you have to have a starting point. Just like Mother Teresa and Alfred Nobel. Each left a legacy, and each had a different way of receiving the calling to give. So, how do you want to be remembered—as a merchant of death or a missionary of charity?

I wrote down everything I wanted and needed in order to make sure my obituary stayed true to its word. I then identified three words that I could use to categorize the tasks I had to accomplish: *portion*, *size*, and *serving*.

The Lord is my portion; therefore, I have hope in Him. In this sense, *portion* means "inheritance." We are the heirs of God's kingdom, as Romans 8:17 tells us, "And if children, then heirs; heirs of God, and joint heirs with Christ; if so be that we suffer with *him*, that we may also be glorified together."

Size refers to magnitude. The size or magnitude of God's grace: "In whom we have redemption through His blood, the forgiveness of sins, according to the riches of His grace … that in the ages to come He might shew the exceeding riches of His grace in *his* kindness toward us through Christ Jesus … Unto me, who am less than the least of all saints, is the grace given, that I should preach among the Gentiles, the unsearchable riches of Christ" (Ephesians 1:7, 2:7, 3:8).

---

76 Washington Post, https://www.washingtonpost.com/wp-srv/inatl/longterm/ teresa/stories/words.htm.

Serving is my daily diet, balanced with His word, which is what I feed on to nourish my heart, soul, and mind each and every day. Deuteronomy 8:3 clearly states that man does not live by bread alone, but man lives by every word that comes from the mouth of the Lord.

I needed to begin with having and understanding all three of these things—portion, size, and serving—in order to pursue a true, fulfilled life with everything that I desired in my life. Use this example: Your life is like a plate. Upon that plate you have daily servings of the Lord's word, which you take in; this feeds your soul, your heart, and your mind, guiding you to carry on God's work and live Christlike each and every day. Each day on that plate the size of God's grace is revealed to you, along with the redemption that is given to you through His blood. It is never ending; it is a gift from God given to us, and it is and should be sufficient. He says His grace is all we need. He works best through weakness. Therefore, boast about your weakness, so that the power of Christ can work through you (2 Corinthians 12:9). Through all this, God is your portion; you rely on Him for all things, He gets you through those things in your life, and your portion is the blessings you have here on earth and the eternal life you are promised in heaven.

But, remember, just as we share in His glory, so must we also share in His suffering. Through baptism, you are baptized into His death. This is the suffering. "Therefore we were buried with him by baptism into death: that like as Christ was raised up from the dead by the Glory of the Father, even so we also should walk in the newness of life." (Romans 6:4–5). That was the main thing I was missing in my life. I never fully died as Christ died. After writing my obituary, reaching the conclusions I came to afterward, and categorizing the aspects of my life accordingly, I then recommitted my life to Christ. I was baptized and finally raised from the dead, and my new life began. That begins as you are raised out of the water. Every day, little by little, everything that I had on my plate was no longer there; I gave God everything that I couldn't deal with. Everything that I messed up I gave to him. My life, my dreams, my work, my money, my kids, my anger, His forgiveness—it all was His. Even my weakness. My life was no longer my own. In return, I got a true life, with clarity, joy, and giving. It was a joy to go back to work again, but most important was the peace within me, knowing that everything—I mean *everything*— that I was experiencing was going to turn out better than I could ever imagine. It may not all turn around overnight, but just knowing that God is my portion, He is all I need, was the crucial first step I needed to take. As soon as I did that, God really started working with me and sending me out on new projects, working through me in a whole new direction. None of this progress happened until I reached out to God and said, "Jesus, help me; I can't do this anymore." There was a sigh of relief; I was no longer alone. He had other people to help and minister to me, and then He revealed to me a way to eat that gave Him glory and me instant relief. A way to get all the nutrients I needed, both spiritually and physically.

I had to start with Christ first before I could start my new program of Eating to Glorify God. If I hadn't done that, my accomplishment would have been in vain. How full is your plate? Is it overflowing with items that God should be handling? Is your plate like that of a Waffle House order: scattered, covered, and smothered? It doesn't have to be. God wants it, but He won't take it unless you give it to Him. *Un*scatter, *un*cover, and *un*smother it all, and reveal to Him everything—your weakness, your pain, your anger—leave nothing unturned. Underneath is nothing left but the "biggie" size of God's grace, His words that are your servings, and the Lord who is and always will be your portion. A day without asking Jesus to help is a day of disorganization, lack of interest and attention, writer's block—you name it; it's a mess. But, stop and pray, "Jesus, help me," and words flow, things open up and run smoothly, and things just get done.

You may actually end up finding yourself writing two obituaries: the one that indicates how you really are, and then a second that reflects how you would really want your obituary to read, thus converting yourself from "Merchant of Death" to "Missionaries of Charity." The difference is all in finding Christ. And then you will find that peace in 1 Corinthians 6:9–11: "Do not be deceived. Neither fornicators, nor idolaters, nor adulterers, nor homosexuals, nor sodomites, nor thieves, nor covetous, nor drunkards, nor revilers, nor extortioners will inherit the kingdom of God. And such were some of you. But you were washed, but you were sanctified, but you were justified in the name of the Lord and by the Spirit of our God." So, you see, that first obituary, well, that was who you were. Say goodbye to the old self, because that is not you anymore.

Several months after I was well into my program and fully living for Christ, I found out quite quickly that God will still test your loyalty. My pastor had given us all a ninety-day challenge in regard to our tithes and offerings. He guaranteed the congregation, trust the Lord in all you do, which includes tithing. Give the exact 10 percent amount, even if you know it is going to hurt your budget; give more as an offering, and always trust in the Lord. Give and have faith that the Lord will provide and blessings will be placed upon us all.

Letters were read at every service, describing how people were blessed and rewarded for their good deeds and their faith in Christ. It was amazing to listen to all the letters. I truly enjoyed hearing them all. I was tithing regularly, and the tithing was actually not a huge challenge for me. Working two jobs and with expenses not that abundant, I never struggled in order to give the full amount, and I did it cheerfully and faithfully. Then, I realized I wasn't truly giving the actual amount that was required, so I increased the amount in order to remain obedient to His word. Still, my budget was not affected. Although my food expenses had increased a bit with my new eating plan, God remained true to His word and still provided me with everything I needed to afford my healthy lifestyle and program of Eating to Glorify God. It wasn't until much later—the ninety days had passed—that I got an amazing answer from God. You see, I have struggled many times with this book. Thinking that maybe this book was just my imagination of success, and it wasn't going to be that great; maybe it was not going to be something that could even be published.

As the days went by, I became more and more successful with my new healthy lifestyle, and it became ever clearer that I was improving each and every day. My head was no longer foggy, I was not bloated, and, within two months, I had already lost fifteen pounds, an amount I had been unable to lose in the recent past; all my pains were gone, no more running to the bathroom, and at each doctor's visit, the medication was decreased instead of increased.

A friend stepped up to the plate and took on my new style of eating. He gave me thirty days to shed the weight. It was actually working for him. Within the first month, he had lost thirteen pounds. He was amazed. I was quite shocked too. On both counts: first, that he stuck with it, and, second, that it actually worked on him as well. People would always ask me, "What can you eat? It seems like you are restricted from almost everything." My response was more supposed to be a comical reply, so, jokingly, I always said, "Well, basically, just what God intended for us to eat."

I still felt led to write this book, and I felt the urge of God pushing me to do so. Yet I would still find myself having ups and downs about this project. What if this was a crazy project of mine that was way over my head, and I would never finish? Just a fad, so to speak. I sometimes thought of myself as one of those people who never really fully succeeded in anything and rarely even finished projects that I'd thought were brilliant ideas, only to conclude that maybe they were just more get-rich-quick, dreaming kind of ideas to live the better life. All those things just never got that perfect push that they needed. So, at times, I found myself wondering if this project was one of those other ideas. Something that only I could see succeeding, but that, in reality would never make it any further than my desk. Then, I would cry to God, "Please let this be what You want it to be. And not be only what I want it to be. If it is only to serve but One and that One is You, then I can accept this. But, God, You know my heart and my desires; I give my worries to You. This book is Yours, have it as You please. Make it become what it is You want it to become. Should it be something that I keep to remind me of what You have done for my life, I will keep it. But should this book be Your words to be read and heard so others who are suffering may no longer suffer, then let Your words speak out through me, and Your will be done." I cried for about fifteen minutes, hoping that my desires, too, would be fulfilled, but I had put my trust in giving this project to Him. It, too, belongs to Him; I was now just a vessel for the work to be done. His timing with this book is His also—something another pastor of mine had advised me.

Later that afternoon, I went to the mailbox to get the mail. I opened a letter and inside that letter was a check for three hundred dollars. My response was cool. I smiled and said, "This is from Jesus." And it was, but it was not a message from Him stating that I had accepted the ninety-day challenge and these were the blessings He was giving back to me. I didn't need the money; remember, God was already blessing me for my faith in Him in my tithing, providing me with the ability to afford the food I needed. This was another message from God, a deeper message. It was an answer to my prayer and my cry to Him from earlier that day (maybe an hour had past). God answered me by saying, "Nothing you do, when you do it to glorify Me, will go unnoticed, and it will never be done in vain." I felt those words strong and clear while I stood holding that check in my hand. By remembering that the Lord is our portion, He is who we inherit, and having full trust in Him, nothing you do will go unnoticed; no prayers will be left unheard. He loves me just as He loves you. Seek Him first, and glorify God in all you do—and then, just be ready to answer the call. And He *will* call upon you. You will never know exactly where it will lead you until you find yourself there. And you will never know exactly how He will respond to your cries and prayers. No matter where you are, He will always be right there with you. Leading you where you need to be, wherever that is on earth. He leads you to serve, and by the time you are done, you may have just served the one thing you strove to do, but chances are you will serve and touch much, much more. The secret to that success is ... *pray.*

Chapter 10

Never Beyond Repair

FTER MOVING FAIRLY QUICKLY through much of the writing this book, I came to a point where everything seemed to halt. No words, no inspiration, nothing. I had nothing else to write and had no clue how to even pick up where I'd left off. I felt terrified and thought that maybe this manuscript would never be published—not because I didn't want to finish it, but because I couldn't finish it. Again, I had talked myself into more worry, but I wasn't moved or shaken just yet.

I was sitting at the table in the kitchen area of the fire station and had placed all the chapters and folders I had been working with onto the tabletop. I then proceeded to place my pink-covered Bible in front of me. Each book in the Bible had its own index tab, and the closed book lay in front of me. I took a deep breath, closed my eyes, and prayed aloud softly, "God, as I open my Bible, show me the words and the verses I need for the chapters to complete this book; give me the wisdom to understand what I am reading and know that it is You who is listening."

Then, I opened my Bible, and the book that I opened it to was Habakkuk. At that very moment, a silent expression went through my mind: *What? Who is this?* I was lost. I had no clue what God was trying to tell me. I must admit another amazing fact of this book that I opened to. I knew nothing of this book, nor had I even read it before. God knew this. So, with an open heart, I began to read. Eventually, I came to chapter 2, the last part of verse 3, the very words that God intended for me to read: "Though it tarry, wait for it; Because it will surely come. It will not tarry." I sat back in my chair, filled with awe.

Habakkuk was a prophet who had a few questions and concerns that he wanted to talk to God about. Habakkuk seemed to be worried about all the violence that was going on. He spoke of the plundering and violence, and even of how powerless the law was and the lack of justice. He cried out to God and raised questions about His plan to deal with all of these problems. So, God replied and told Habakkuk of His plan. The nation that God was raising up He described as an evil and a bitter nation. God even said they were terrible and dreadful. They would ride on "horses swifter than leopards and more fierce than evening wolves." But I did not get the impression that Habakkuk liked God's reply; nor did he like the nation that God would be using to get rid of these problems. So, God had to show His patience once again. He had Habakkuk write a vision on a tablet: "For the vision is yet for an appointment time, But at the end it shall speak; and not lie. Though it tarry, wait for it. because it will surely come, it will not tarry. Behold, His soul which is lifted up is not upright in him; but the just shall live his faith" (Habakkuk 2:3–4).

Habakkuk was terrified and concerned for the people; it almost seemed like maybe he was thinking that God wasn't listening to him or wasn't trying to do anything to give him relief in the midst of his plight. God was listening, though; He even took the time to reply to Habakkuk by telling him His plans. But could you imagine the shock if the cavalry that is sent to help you is even more evil than what is heading your way? I could very well see the concern. It would be like fighting fire with fire, and the problem would only get bigger. That seemed to be what Habakkuk thought. But God comforts Habakkuk, easing his fears, saying, essentially, "Have faith; I've got this. Don't rush into anything. My plans for you will come, and it won't be long."

So, Habakkuk had to remind himself that no matter what might happen and what might lie ahead, he had to maintain his faith and trust in the Lord. We see that he did so in chapter 3, verses 17–19: "Although the fig tree shall not blossom, neither shall fruit be in the vines, the labour of the olive shall fail, and the fields shall yield no meat; the flock shall be cut off from the fold, and there shall be no herd in the stalls—Yet I will rejoice in the Lord. I will joy in the God of my salvation. The Lord God is my strength, and He will make my feet like hinds' feet, and He will make me walk upon high places. To the chief singer on my stringed instruments."

You may—and probably will—find that God's plans aren't exactly what you had in mind, nor do they usually present themselves in the way you feel you would like to handle them, but all God asks is that we have faith that all will come together and it will fit and it will without a doubt turn out for the better. The result will be that you will praise God for what He has done for you and how He has answered your questions and concerns.

Nevertheless, I admit that I still couldn't really figure out how all this played a part in writing this book, much less another chapter. So, I took the book of Habakkuk, chapter 2, verse 3, and I tried every which way I could think of to include it in the chapter that had me stumped—even if only to begin my chapter with this verse. I plugged it in every which way I could, but I still didn't feel the feeling I normally got when writing a chapter, which was that I was on target. It just wasn't flowing. I was stumped and at the point of writer's block. So I stopped. I saved what I had written and set it aside.

For a week, nothing happened. Then, my friend asked me how my book was coming along; he had noticed I had not really put much effort into it lately. I told him I had writer's block, but I assured him that things would pick up again and the book would still happen. I said I had really just kind of taken a hiatus from it, hoping that a break would help; maybe I'd just been thinking too hard and trying too hard.

He then asked me if I wanted to go with him to go get a new pair of running shoes. We had this one store where we liked to go, and I like to shop when there is a mission. I agreed to go and was actually looking forward to the trip. A good opportunity to walk away, get out from under it all, and take a nice break. I liked the way the associates at this store helped you shop for the perfect running shoe. They used state-of-the-art machines to test how you stood on your feet, and then they watched you run, and the machines calculated how you ran. I loved the scientific approach of selecting the perfect running shoe for your feet. (I wish there was a system or machine that could automatically find the perfect shoe for every dress. I have always had better results finding the shoe first, then searching for the outfit—but that is for another book!) Once the machines have calculated the pertinent data, the associates bring out five or six different brands to help you select the right one for you. It is like choosing an apple. They are all apples, but each apple is a different type, like the Granny Smith, the Red Delicious, and so on. Call it what you want, but they are still apples! In this case, the apples are running shoes. With running shoes, each brand has its own approach to the shoe, so you have to find which brand works best for your feet and match that with your running habits and needs. As he was trying on each shoe, my friend and the sales associated walked outside to take a quick run while my friend wore the possible purchase to test it. They struck up a conversation about how my friend got into running, and he told the other guy the story about changing his eating habits with my new eating lifestyle ideas. The guy was intrigued, so my friend told him that I was writing a book about it.

This was the day; today was the day God revealed to me my new chapter.

The sales associate then came back into the store to talk to me. This man looked to about my age: forty-five or so. He was relatively young and appeared to be healthy; you would have never imagined that he was ever sick, much less afflicted with the tragic story of disease and disappointment that he was about to relate to me. He sat down with me while my friend continued to try on each shoe brand. He began by saying, "I'd like to tell you a story."

I will now tell you what he told me. In 2009, he was diagnosed with a virus in his heart. That virus manifested into congestive heart failure, which later caused him to need to have a pacemaker inserted. (He showed us the four-inch lump on the left side of his chest, just below his collarbone, where the pacemaker was.) By the time most people would have accepted the blow that this condition had placed upon them, he was taking six different prescription pills and telling himself that he was not going to allow this condition to dictate his life and his goals. Before the illness, he had been a marathon runner and a triathlon competitor. He'd had a body of steel with a heart of iron—and gold. He had claimed his victory and was not settling for anything less. His diet became similar to that of the Paleo Diet, consisting mostly of lean meats, fruits, and vegetables. As the months and years went by, his doctors reduced his medications and allowed him to increase his running distances. Later, he returned to being a marathon runner and the triathlon competitor, but with another ambition: Ironman. Before the Ironman competition came around, he was completely off all prescription medications, and his doctors were now contemplating removing the pacemaker. The pacemaker readings were sent via computer, so the doctors saw how is heart was functioning and working under the stress and exertions it was subjected to. The test readings were remarkable and blew the minds of the doctors. They described him as "the healthiest man with a pacemaker." But, during a competition, his pacemaker went off. Whether it was accidental or justifiable, the man telling his story was not moved or shaken by the occurrence; he saw it as a minor setback that would lead to his greatest comeback. His last Ironman competition went perfectly, without incident, and the doctors were now reconsidering the removal of his pacemaker.

Now, I did not ask how he placed in the competition; I didn't really feel that placement was important. His overall victory in his endeavor against the odds was all that mattered. I thanked him for sharing his story, and his humbleness proved to me that he would not have done anything different; he even seemed to feel honored to have a story that he could tell an interested listener like me. I was just as honored to hear the amazing story and found myself feeling so blessed that God had chosen this man to tell his story to me.

Let me explain all this a bit further so that you will see why this led me back to the chapter I had so struggled with. Congestive heart failure (CHF) is a disease that affects nearly 6 million Americans,[77] and about 670,000 people are diagnosed with CHF each year.[78] This disease does not mean that your heart has stopped completely; rather, it is a disease where your heart is not pumping normally, and so the blood is not adequately circulated throughout your body.[79] When blood is not pumped properly throughout the body, oxygen cannot be moved; therefore, nutrients, including oxygen, cannot meet the needs of the body. For various reasons—coronary artery disease, infections, alcohol or drug abuse, even thyroid disease and diabetes, and let's not forget the common heart attack—the walls of the heart become weakened, and then the fluid does not move smoothly. As with cars in a traffic jam, fluid gets backed up because the kidneys are responding to the need to retain the water and salt as a result of the heart's inability to pump effectively, and then fluid begins to build in the arms, legs, ankles, lungs, and other organs. Hence, the body becomes congested. You become short of breath because the lungs back up with fluid. You get dizzy, tired, and weak because there in less blood in your major organs, including your brain; your heartbeat becomes fast or irregular, working faster to pump the blood. CHF is often a progressive condition and it usually develops in people with the high

77 American Heart Association, "What Is Heart Failure?" Answers by Heart, 2015, https://www.heart.org/-/media/data-import/downloadables/pe-abh-what-is-congestive-heart-failure-ucm_300315.pdf.

78 John E. Blair, Mark Huffman, and Sanjiv J Shah, "Cardiology Review: Heart Failure in North America," May 9, 2013, https://www.ncbi.nlm.nih.gov/pmc/articles/PMC3682397/.

79 American Heart Association, "Congestive Heart Failure and Congenital Defects," Health Topics, http://www.heart.org/en/health-topics/congenital-heart-defects/the-impact-of-congenital-heart-defects/congestive-heart-failure-and-congenital-defects.

risks mentioned earlier. WebMD advises that you can prevent CHF from worsening by keeping your blood pressure low, monitoring your own symptoms, maintaining fluid balance, limiting salt intake, monitoring your weight and losing weight if needed, monitoring new symptoms, taking your medications, and seeing your doctor regularly. With the right care, CHF does not have to stop you from doing the things you enjoy, but it is up to you to make the changes necessary to either one day walk away from CHF and be CHF-free (like my new friend did), or live with CHF and accept the cards that you have been dealt.

The greatest gift you can give your body is the gift of health. The gift of the best nutrients and minerals it was meant to have; the pure essentials necessary for your body to function at its maximum capacity. We want the most we can get out of our cars; we use the best oil, the best tires, and whatever it takes to keep it running longer—and, for some, faster. I did. As I've mentioned, I was one of those who worked on my own car. There were very few things I did not attempt on my own when it came time to maintaining my car and doing necessary repairs. I changed my own oil, brakes, and tires. I even went as far as changing the alternator belt and O_2 sensors. I tackled it all. My Ford SUV had nearly three hundred thousand miles on it when I drove to Atlanta and for the very first time since owning this car. Well, it left me on the side of the road. It wouldn't start. It wasn't out of gas, so I had no choice but to call AAA and have my car towed. I had been lucky with this car; everything that ever had gone wrong with it had always been simple, and I'd never had a major repair done on my car. I used to tell people that this car and I had a deal, an agreement so to speak: all I asked was that it get me through while all my girls were in college. That technically amounted to about five years. And maybe that deal would have been reachable if they hadn't changed majors and then gotten married. The last one will be finishing this year, seeking to get her master's. But there I was sitting in the waiting room, waiting for the "doctor" to come out and tell me the good news. It seemed to be the longest thirty minutes I had ever lived through. It broke my heart to see my little black SUV with the firefighter tag in front on top of a rollback wrecker. Then, in the background, barely coming over the loudspeaker, I heard my name called. I stood up and walked toward the counter, and the man's face had the look of not good news but bad news. My car was dead. It was beyond repair.

In life, when we are diagnosed with a chronic disease, such as CHF, Crohn's, diabetes, and so forth, it is common to conclude that a lot of medication and constant treatment and management will be included in your daily routine. Most people will become depressed and cease to be active, and they may even have very little desire to live. Some would rather die. Others might reach the conclusion that the damage is done, and there is no reversing it. But, what if, with a change in eating habits, your body will and does begin to heal itself? We have all seen scratches, bumps, cuts, and bruises heal on our bodies, and we did nothing to make the healing happen. The body took on its natural ability to make itself whole again, and sometimes no scar will even remain. If it can do that on the outside, what would keep it from making those changes and healing you from within? No matter where you are in your illness—in the beginning, or heading to the final stage—you are never beyond repair, and you can make your health status better. There are so many benefits from eating those herbs, fresh fruits and vegetables, and other whole foods. The healing power within you is boosted and magnified when you eat the foods that God originally intended for us to eat. The examples are great, and there are too many to mention them all, but let's list some just so you will understand why eating these plant foods is so important to our health today:

To lower blood pressure, eat bananas and other potassium-rich foods, including cayenne, raisins, kiwi, purple potatoes, watermelon, chocolate, and garlic.

To lower cholesterol, have avocados, lentils, edamame, nuts, olive oil, pears, green and black tea, and a tomato.

To lower blood sugar, consume lima beans, oatmeal, granola, peanuts and peanut butter, tofu, vinegar, cinnamon, grapefruit, and spinach.

To reduce inflammation (which includes leaky gut syndrome), eat berries, kiwi, citrus fruits, olives and olive oil, dark leafy greens, salmon (all sources of omega-3).

To fight acid reflux, have oatmeal, ginger, aloe vera, salads (greens), banana, melons, fennel, cauliflower, broccoli, asparagus, and green beans.

The list goes on. ...

Honey can increase calcium absorption, help with arthritic joints, fight colds, and boost ulcer healing. It helps with constipation, acting as a natural, gentle laxative. It can help with allergies and obesity, and serves an antibiotic in treatments for gangrene, surgical wound infections, and incisions. It has also been used to protect skin grafts, corneas, blood vessels, and bones during storage and shipment, according to www.naturalnews.com. Alfalfa can help in rebuilding body cells; artichoke aids in bloodstream nourishment; broccoli maintains the water balance of your body; cabbage can also treat stomach ulcers; celery helps the body to rid itself of carbon dioxide; mustard greens help build capillaries; okra helps with intestinal disorders; onion aids with gastric-tract stimulation; radishes soothe the nerves and cleanse and purify your bloodstream. All according to www.rethinkingcancer.org.

Those who ate processed foods and then changed their lifestyle, eating all natural, fresh fruits and vegetables and less meat, showed significant positive changes in their bodies. Lower blood pressure, reduced cholesterol, decreased body weight, improved focus and clarity, reduced inflammation, healed digestive tracts, and reversed malabsorption. The positive results are endless. Each and every time, the body responded positively to the changes. Everyone benefits from this change.

There is always a point where it is possible to overcome your disease and illness, making that positive difference in your health. You are never so beyond repair that eating fruits and vegetables will not make some kind of positive difference in your life. It is a reconstruction that you will be grateful you undertook because of the extended life you were given and the energy you received. Your body will thank you in ways that everyone will notice. Your doctor may not understand it when the tests show that the cancer cells are reducing or the pacemaker can be removed or you are improving in terms of whatever ails you, but he or she will still be pleased. With a smile, the doctor will tell you, "The only advice I can give you is to keep doing what you are doing."

Change and answers will come. God knows your questions and hears your prayers. Like Habakkuk *"though it may tarry"* be patient and see what God reveals to you.

Chapter 11

Setback? Comeback!

WE CELEBRATE IN EVERYTHING we do. When we celebrate, we tend to use food and alcohol as the means of celebrating. Friends and family will always be around to share that celebration with you. For example, when you go to a friend and are so excited because you finally lost those first five pounds, some of your friends will be the first ones to step up and help you find those pounds you lost. And they will, because we celebrate that accomplishment with the same thing we were struggling with: food. You have that cake, all that fatty food. Everyone is happy. The food is great and tastes so good; you are in the comfort zone, and the serotonin is peaking in your brain. You think you are in control. The next thing you know, those five pounds are back.

When I was working with a private ambulance service on one of my days off, we responded to a call: a gentleman had fallen out of his bedroom window. The window was not that high up, maybe fifteen feet. There were several bushes below to break his fall, so what could have resulted in several broken bones, enabled him to walk away with just a few scratches and, undoubtedly, soreness that would linger for a few days. When we arrived on the scene, he was up and walking around. It was obvious he had been drinking—a lot. It was barely after 12:00 noon, but, just as a precaution, my partner and I put him on the backboard and took him to the hospital for further evaluation.

But, before we left to head to the hospital, I asked him, "How in the world did you manage to fall out of the window?"

His reply was quite simple: "I was celebrating." He was laughing and smiling. He was so happy.

Then, I asked him, "Celebrating what?"

He said, "I was celebrating my sobriety."

It is usually not until the next day, after that celebration, that we realize we made a wrong turn and now find ourselves right back in the same situation we were trying to get ourselves out of. Then, all those depressing emotions begin to set in. The feelings of inadequacy, frustration, and downright defeat. These are all sure signs of emotional failure. What if we didn't look at these as failures, but, instead, as a journey that has yet to be completed. It is still under development, and it is only a minor setback along the path to success. But, in order to get back on that path, you have to truly find out what went wrong. Why did you make these choices that led you to this wall, this obstacle, basically right back where you started?

We have all been there, and there are times when we have said, "I just can't do it" or "I don't know how to do it." Or, "This is my life and it's just the way it is; this is the hand I was dealt." All these statements are very powerful self-denials of empowerment. But what if all that could change? What if you could do it? What if you discovered how to do it? What if that deck of cards you have been dealt was suddenly no longer in your hands?

What if you couldn't fail?

There were so many people in the Bible who had setbacks, just as we do today. Abraham and Sarah were burdened for many years with not being able to conceive a child. They both were well beyond the age of even thinking about giving birth to a child, even though the deepest desire of them both was to have a son. And through all the disappointments, and despite any and all obstacles, Abraham's willingness to obey God, his continuance to walk in faith, not only provided a miracle that only the Lord could give him—a son, Isaac— but God also made Abraham the father of many nations. These were all promises made and kept by God. "And the Scripture was fulfilled which says, Abraham believed God, and it was imputed unto him for righteousness. And he was called the Friend of God" (James 2:23).

Abraham knew that God was in control of his life. Abraham found that the best way to handle any situation was to allow God to maintain that very control that He wanted and had. Could you imagine the drastic change in history if Abraham had just taken it upon himself to manage his life and basically told God, "It's okay, God; I can take it from here." Abraham maintained his control by allowing God to be in control. Giving up that control can be very difficult for some of us. But we have to realize that if we do not allow God to maintain control of our lives, we are just setting are ourselves up to fail. And that failure didn't ever have to happen, and wouldn't happen if we just trusted God.

When I was young, my parents often took us kids on vacation. My dad seemed to always love to stop at those rest areas off the interstate. It always seemed like a good place to stop and stretch your legs and take care of other needs, whether it was using the bathroom or getting something to drink. It was a safe place as well. Not many people would be around, so we kids could run off our energy. As I grew older and began to travel on my own, those rest areas became a stress-free zone and safe haven for me, just as they had for my parents. They offered a way to get away from the traffic or just take a break from the long road that seemed to be leading to nowhere. One particular day, I opted for the rest area to get away from the traffic that had been backed up for miles from a wreck that had occurred even further up the road. I was frustrated; I needed to get my destination at a certain time, and this was going to delay me even more. So, I opted to get off and spend some time at a rest area. Just as my luck would have it, the rest area was closed. I then had no choice but to sit through all that traffic and go through the suffering of stop-and-go traffic. There was no resting, just sitting idle. I had to see it through, and when I came to where the traffic started to open up, astounding joy filled me, and "Thank You, Jesus" came out of my mouth.

Isn't that the way life is? As Christians, when we come to a blocking moment in our lives and we just want to get to a rest area, hoping it all just passes by and then we can pick it up from there just so we don't have to deal with what is lying ahead of us, what we need to do is call on God. In order to deal with those sudden setbacks, we can't just pull over and sit idle. The rest area is closed. You have to find a way to move forward and keep on going. That is what God wants us to do. Don't give up. If you do pull over, all you will have done is create a longer journey to find the end result of the success within you.

We all have to come to the realization that the rest area is closed in some aspects of life. You cannot rest and sit idle at any time. In times of death, sadness, and disappointments, in order to find success—especially the working miracles of God—you have to keep moving. God works through us constantly. There is never a moment that He stops to take a break, so why should we? Job praised God no matter what happened to him. Job was a man who was truly dedicated to God. Then, the Devil got permission to tempt Job, which God allowed, but with the stipulation that the Devil could not kill him. Job lost his family and his wealth, and boils covered his body. Job never cursed God. His friends and wife tried to get Job to curse God, but he didn't. He couldn't. He always remained loyal to God and praised Him for everything. After the temptations were over, God blessed Job with twice as much as what he'd had before. At no time did Job think about pulling off the road, waiting in a rest area, and sitting idle. Like Abraham, Job knew God was in control. He understood that this, too, shall pass. He never even thought about taking any control over his life and all those tormenting situations. Because of his faith and patience, Job was rewarded, and he prevailed. His setback became his greatest comeback.

When I was going through my ordeal of seeing doctors and more doctors, taking medicine and more medicine, and with nothing changing or getting better, I felt great despair. I'd eat badly, and I would hurt. I'd eat well, and I would hurt. Nothing was working. It seemed everything changed when I got baptized. That was the true point in my life when I gave God all control. I had sat idle too long and was at the point of almost giving up. God was trying to show me that I was on the right track when it came to healing my body through food. But it wasn't until I started listening that He showed me I needed His help 100 percent in order to get better. Once I did exactly what He expected of me—which included eating all natural, whole foods and very minimally processed foods—my body start to make a complete 360-degree turnaround.

As I mentioned, I always made jokes when people asked me, "So what can you eat?" Who would have thought that my humorous reply, "Basically, only that which God intended," would actually prove true! Little did I know it would become such a huge breakthrough for me. I had to start from the very beginning, to find my areas in which I went wrong, and then move to correct them. My first point of contact was with God, then the Bible. From then, things began to become even clearer. I could focus, I was able to sleep, and never again would I have to worry about where the restrooms were. I was even losing weight. But it didn't stop there. I knew that this success was from God. I had to keep moving and not sit idle in response to this huge change in my life. My success continues to drive me to want to be even better, to please God and praise Him for all He has accomplished in me. I am so grateful that I got sick. Without that, I would have never looked up and seen that Jesus was there—and He was there the whole time. He was just waiting on me, just like He is waiting on you. Every time you stumble, He will be there to pick you and help you start over again.

I read somewhere once that some successes can only come through experiencing those setbacks and that setbacks are opportunities to see God in action. So, sitting idle means you are missing out and putting off the moment of your success. It will also mean that you will miss out on what God can truly do for you and through you. So, when you fall back and gain those pounds back, or reach over again for the bottle, give that control back to God. Let Him be the one you reach for.

Tell Him you cannot do this without Him and that He is in control. Without Him, we will surely fail. Through Him, realize that all things are possible. The Devil is the one who wants us to fail. You have to keep on trying. By giving God all that is weak, it will make you stronger. When it does come time to celebrate your success, celebrate through Jesus. Give Him the glory. Reach out to Jesus, not the bottle or that piece of cake. Because when you do get that setback that urges you to drink or to eat more than you should—or when you are overwhelmed by a setback with whatever struggles you may have—if you give in, you are taking that control back from God. You are telling God, "I can take it from here." Instead, you should always remember that Jesus died for you and me on the cross. He went to the gates of hell and took back control, and He has the key. He rose to the heavens, and now He lives, and He lives inside me and you. Since Jesus can do all that, why wouldn't you want to have Him in control of your life?

Hebrews 12:1–3 states:

> "Wherefore, seeing we also are compassed about with so great a cloud of witnesses, let us lay aside every weight, and the sin which doth so easily beset us, and let us run with patience the race that is set before us, [2] Looking unto Jesus, the author and finisher of our faith; who for the joy that was set before him endured the cross, despising the shame, and set down at the right hand of the throne of God. [3] For consider him who endured such contradiction of sinners against himself, lest ye be wearied and lose faint in your minds."

It doesn't get much clearer than that. Give God the control and glory over all. Take nothing back. It was not yours to have in the first place. Through prayer, there is always hope. From CHF to triathlon to Ironman. What will be your greatest comeback?

Chapter 12

Water to Wine

L ET'S TALK ABOUT WATER, also known as H_2O, hydrogen and two oxygens combined and connected with covalent bonds. This tasteless and odorless chemical compound of no calories and no organic nutrients is an essential substance for humans and all forms of life. It covers nearly 70 percent of the earth's surface, and 70 percent of the human body is comprised of water as well. The compound is so diverse that it can be frozen, boiled, and even vaporized (steam); it can also take the shape of whatever it is contained in.

Water functions with many uses, including drinking, washing, cooking, agriculture, transportation, chemical process, heat exchange, recreation, fire extinguishing, processing foods, and, of course, dieting. Water consumption is one of the most important tools you will need to successfully—and healthfully—lose weight and then maintain your ideal weight. Water helps to eliminate toxins, bring nutrients to your cells, and aid with preventing dehydration. Without water, your survival rate will decrease, and death can occur within two to ten days. Water is a metabolic booster as well as a natural appetite suppressant. Consuming water prior to meals has been known to reduce the need or desire to overeat. Insufficient intake of water could result in weight gain because your body will go into "survival mode" and retain water to maintain the level of hydration your body needs. It is recommended by all doctors and nutritionists that at least eight glasses of water, or one cup (eight ounces) per pound of weight is necessary for your body to function at its best. However, if you are more of an active person, your intake requirement may be greater in order to maintain your hydration.

Water is mentioned in the Bible more than seven hundred times. But what is even more interesting is that it is first mentioned in Genesis and last in Revelation. "In the beginning, God created the heaven and earth, And the earth was without form, and void; and darkness was upon the face of the deep. And the Spirit of God moved upon the face of the waters" (Genesis 1:1–2 KJV). It was not until the second day that land was placed on the earth and "it divided the waters from the waters." In Revelation, the Bible brings to us the visions of the apostle John, when "the third angel poured out his vial upon the rivers and fountains of waters; and they became blood"(Revelation 16:4 KJV).

Water has always been a significant source and symbol in our Christian walk of faith. Without water, the soul will surely die and perish. Water is the symbol of the Holy Spirit, often referred to as the Water of Life. Revelation 21:6 tells us, "He said unto me: 'It is done. I am Alpha and O-meg-a, the beginning and the end. I will give unto him that is athirst of the fountain of the water of life freely.'"

Wanting and needing more from Jesus drives a thirst in you that can only be quenched by the Holy Spirit. You obtain this thirst from being baptized in the water, your soul cleansed and your body new and reborn to a new life with Jesus Christ as your Savior. This is the final link and connection that I found to Jesus when I accepted Him into my life. Without it, my life was missing purpose and timing. Something was always wrong within me, and I never could figure out what that was. Then, as I've shared, my pastor gave a class and instructed us on the meaning of baptism and what it was truly about. I had what I've described as my aha moment. I had been baptized, but I'd never taken that deep, cleansing plunge into a bath filled with the Water of Life. It was a commitment, a way to seal the deal that I belonged to Him, and my life was no longer mine. It also became my announcement to the church and the congregation that I was fully in Christ; I needed Christ, and I needed the church too.

Baptism was the first step of my journey as a witness to Jesus Christ, my Lord and Savior. I walked with Jesus and talked with Jesus. It was my duty to minister about Jesus and be Christlike for the rest of my time here on this earth. All through my life up to that point, I had thought that I was true to Jesus and my family. But I wasn't. I hadn't fully committed to Him. But, when I did, the power of Him opened up from the heavens and filled me with love and joy. Most importantly, I had peace. Just like the song says, "Signed, sealed, and delivered, I am yours." Instead, though, it is signed, sealed, delivered; I am His. I signed up my life to be all for Christ. I sealed it with baptism, and my soul was delivered unto Him. And then, for the first time, I was truly saved and free from everything. It was the happiest day of my life. The connection that brought me to Jesus brought more energy to be released within me. My desires became His. My jobs and projects are His. My head became clearer. My burdens and worries? Yep, they are now His. I was no longer thirsty, and my desire was to be as close as I could be with Jesus. Because I was no longer in control of my life, God became my controller. And I told Him that He could have it all, because all I was doing was messing it up without letting Him be my commander. Water washes those toxins out of your body and keeps you clean. The Water of Life, through Jesus Christ, will wash away your sins and cleanse your soul.

Just like we need water in the beginning and the end, we need Jesus from the beginning to the end as well. Without it, everything turns to mud. Mud is thick and bogs you down. You can't move through it at all without some form of difficulty. It makes your legs heavy and your body weak to the point of exhaustion. You become angry because you can't get through it. Sometimes, as you walk through this mud, you take another step, and you drop down fast and hard. You find yourself in way too deep. The further you move through the mud, the deeper it gets; your legs become heavy and bogged down, as if you were in quicksand. It does not have to be this way. I have never seen a situation controlled with mud that works out well. The harder you try to move to get unstuck, the more stuck you become. Instead, dive into new waters, cleaner water—accept Jesus Christ into your heart. Let Him wash you clean with the Holy Spirit, with the Water of Life, through baptism. Give your life to Him. He can and will lift you out of that muddy, murky place in your life. He can and will give you a clean new life. He will pick you up and help you grow. You will become a light to shine so that others will see and want to follow. His burden is light, and His yoke is easy. Leave the mud for those four-wheel-drive vehicles. Walk with Jesus; follow Him. I do, because I can't walk on water; nor can I walk through mud.

Wine

Wine has a long history of use as a form of medication, a digestive aid, and a safe alternative to drinking water. It dates back to 2200 BC, making it the oldest documented man-made medicine. Wine continued to play a role in medicine up to the late nineteenth and early twentieth centuries, which, because of research, changed when health concerns arose with alcohol and alcoholism. Studies showed a link between a variety of diseases, such as hypertension, cancer, liver damage, strokes, and infertility, just to mention a few. They also showed a connection between the consumption of alcohol by pregnant mothers and mental retardation in children, all part of fetal alcohol syndrome. It wasn't until the late twentieth and early twenty-first centuries that wine made a comeback, with reevaluations suggesting that moderate consumption of wine played a healthy role. In 1990, for example, new studies revealed the health benefits of wine: through moderate consumption, it could actually result in lower occurrences of cardiovascular disease, which could reduce the risks of heart attacks. According to an article in www.foodandwine. com, moderate wine consumption cuts the risk of colon cancer, cataracts, and type 2 diabetes, slows down the rate of brain decline, and could promote longevity. Studies have also revealed that an antioxidant called resveratrol, which occurs in wine, helps prevent damage to the blood vessels in the heart, prevents blood clots, and reduces bad cholesterol. So, who wouldn't drink to that?

Stressing moderate consumption, wine will also not create those awful sugar spikes that you a trying to avoid while dieting. But you have to be careful, because it will lower your blood sugar, and it can stimulate your appetite, which may result in overeating. But how much wine is just enough? First, let's mention the obvious. If you are stumbling, you have had way too much. Even "tipsy" is a result of having too much. I am a true advocate of even if you have had just one glass of any alcohol-based drink, do not drive. I must also advise that drunkenness is a sin, and this reduces the health benefits that come with wine. I have a feeling that the term *moderate consumption* took the front seat to a glass of wine each day. It became a loophole. Maybe to some people the definition of a glass became that of something closer to the size of a fishbowl. Wineglasses come in many sizes and shapes. They are intended for each different type of wine, and the class of wine determines which glass it is served in. It goes back to being a wine taster, the advocate, and the aromas that particular glass will emit from the wine. Each particular glass that is chosen for the wine will provide a deeper appreciation and better experience that is intended by the consumer and the makers of each particular wine. So, a daily recommendation for wine is considered to be a five-ounce glass for women and no more than two drinks for men, according to an article in Healthy Eating, in 2018.[80] In moderation and to maintain safety and effectiveness, cheers! Enjoy the benefits of the wine.

80 Alissa Fleck, "The Recommended Alcohol Intake per Week," Healthy Eating | SF Gate, http://healthyeating.sfgate.com/recommended-alcohol-intake-per-week-5280.html, accessed October 19, 2018.

Water to Wine

Marriage at Cana is a story well known as the first miracle that Jesus performed, described in the Gospel of John. Jesus and His mother, the Virgin Mary, along with His disciples, were invited to a wedding, and when the wine ran out, Jesus turned the water into wine. This story manifested many outcomes and was just the beginning of many more miracles to come. But there was more to this story than just a miracle. It brought me to a moment of who Jesus truly is and what others became in light of this amazing feat. As you read the scripture you come to a part where Mary is frantic. The wedding party is out of wine. I can feel the worry she would have. I know when my daughter was married we had planned for maybe two hundred people. But four hundred arrived, maybe even more. Within twenty minutes of serving the food, the beef sandwiches were devoured, and the punch was empty. It was a nightmare arising, and there was nothing we could do. We had brought only what was bought. There was no more to provide. It is a scary feeling. You worry years later that guests reflect on the wedding only to remember that there was no food or drinks left on that very special occasion, your daughter's wedding day. So, when Mary approached Jesus about her concern, He said something so powerful, and it put me in a place of peace and comfort. Jesus said, "Woman, what have I to do with thee? Mine hour is not yet come" (John 2:4). My hour has not come. We find so much patience in this story. You see, time belongs to Jesus. He has a season and a moment for all things. And until we are truly ready to accept His patience, some things will not pass nor happen in the time that you think they may happen or that you want them to happen. As followers of Christ, we have to learn that patience, not rushing what is perfect in Him. For Jesus knows what is best and when it is best to receive those blessings and needs we seek from Him. Jesus could have created the water to turn into wine that very second, but He waited. He waited for an hour. How many times have we all lost patience with someone, waiting on them for what may have only been fifteen minutes! We get upset, we lose control of our emotions, and sometimes we may even leave without continuing to wait for that person. Jesus waited for that perfect hour and perfect moment to perform just one of His greatest miracles. Yet, Jesus waits even longer, for some of us—He is patient, preciously patient. He knew what it would take to make that wine from water. He changed a tasteless, odorless liquid, turning it into a sweet wine. The master of the banquet did not even know where the wine came from. Jesus had transformed a nothing, something ordinary, to something spectacular and something that no one had ever had before. He did this with patience. Is that not what Jesus does with us? Once we ask him to come into our lives, He changes each and every one of us into something spectacular, something new to you and everyone else who is around you. He did it with patience and timing. He waited on you until that very moment when you knew you could not go on any longer and then you came to Him and asked Him for help. Jesus waits patiently on that hour for us to seek His love, and then He transforms us, just like He transformed the wine from water.

But the story does not stop there. In chapter 2, verse 9 of the Gospel of John, the master of the banquet tastes the water that had been turned into wine. He didn't know where the wine had come from, so he told the bridegroom, obviously with pleasing approval, that everyone usually brings out the best choice of wine first, but he had saved the best till now. I feel he had to be thinking, *How genius is that?!* I would have thought the same thing. So, with that, I discovered another attribute of Jesus: what He does is not second best or of lower quality. What He gives us is that of only true high-quality, first-class treatment. I was cleaning a house one day, a house that I had been cleaning for nearly eleven years. The owner of the home was rarely there. But when he did spend some days there, I would always place fresh sheets on the bed. Well, each time I changed the sheets, the next time he stayed the night, I would always notice that the sheets were pulled up to the extent that what had been tucked between the two mattresses was almost pulled up completely to the top of the bed. The bed always looked like there had been a massive, brutal fight with the sheets, and someone lost. I would remake the bed the exact same way as I had done before and continue on with my work. Years went by. Then, finally, something just hit me: maybe there was a need for more sheets, the owner, who was rather tall, was trying to pull more of the sheets up for better cover. I tried to adjust, but, each and every time, the bed always looked like a battle had gone on. Finally, he came to me, and all he had to do was mention the word *sheets*, and I knew what he was talking about. For ten-plus years, I had been short sheeting him and did not realize it. Now I can see the struggle of a six-foot, two-inch man trying to get more sheets to cover up under on a bed that was made for a five-foot, three-inch person. I often laugh about it now. Together, we corrected the problem, and he was never short sheeted again. That is Jesus: no matter what, it is always first-class love, and you will never be short sheeted in anything. Jesus wants the best for us, and, therefore, He will always give us the best. That hour will be ours if we would just wait and listen to Him and do what He asks of us. It is so simple—a transformation that can only be completed with His help and can only be done through Him.

The Gospel of John, chapter 2, verse 11, we read, "This beginning of miracles did Jesus in Cana of Galilee and manifested forth his glory; and his disciples believed in him." When we discover what Jesus can do for our lives through His transformation of us, we, too, shall believe—and you will. Then and only then will you come to believe the patience, and the glory of Jesus and the transformation He has in store for you. He will change it right before your eyes and through you; you will bring more people to have faith and believe in Him. In order to obtain those blessings of healing and gifts from the Water of Life, God asks of us to walk in faith and believe. Have faith in Him so that his work will come through. Mary tells the servants in verse 5, "Whatever he saith unto you, do it." Mary had enough faith that when Jesus told her to wait, she waited. So, we need to have that very same belief. No matter what Jesus asks us to do, we, too, should have that faith and do all things that He commands us to do. Believe as the disciples did, have faith like Mary did, serve as the servants served, and have the patience of Jesus and—know that time belongs to Jesus and that hour is yours and is now for the having. You just have to ask. Ask Him to come into your heart and be your personal Savior, and believe that He is.

I have to no reason to believe that Mary did not run to Jesus for help. I could have used that fish miracle for my daughter's wedding, feeling nervous and anxious and needing to solve this dilemma. I don't think there was anyone else Mary could turn too. So, she asked, just like Jesus asks of us. He wants us to ask for help. Just like the man in Mark 10:17, who ran up to Jesus and fell on his knees before him asking him, "Good master, what shall I do that I may inherit eternal life?" Jesus told him to keep His commandments, and the man replied that he had done all that since he was a boy. Then, Jesus told him to "sell whatsoever thou hast and give to the poor, and thou shalt have treasure in heaven; and come take up the cross, and follow me."

Running to Jesus is one thing, but then, just like any pastor will tell us, you have to listen to what Jesus is saying and then do as He asks. That is what He asks of us all. Just like when Jesus told the servants to fill the jars with water. They did exactly what was expected of them. I am sure they had no clue what was to happen next. Could you imagine what the servants were thinking at that time? Maybe something like *Oh, this is going to go over well. These jars were last filled with wine. The guests are expecting more wine, and we have only water.* The fear must have raged inside them; they must have been terrified of disappointing the guests and possibly having an irate crowd. But they did exactly what was asked of them. Just like Mary told them to do. No questions. They obeyed and followed Mary's instructions precisely. Isn't that the way we should be? With all the patience Jesus has for us, and the hour that He waits for us to have. Yet we ask why, or we may not even take the time to listen for his instructions, instead just doing things we want to do in our own way. Some of us don't even know He is waiting. But He is. He is waiting patiently for that very hour—the hour that He has reserved especially for you, that very hour that brings you to that transformation from tasteless to sweet. It is the first miracle that Jesus creates in us all. He transforms us from sin to forgiveness, and then He saves us from the life of destruction we were headed toward. Run to him; He is patiently waiting.

Chapter 13

D.I.E.T
(Diligence in Every Thing)

D IET ... THAT FOUR-LETTER WORD that everyone hates to use. I asked my daughter to help me sum up the word diet and maybe create a better acronym for the letters. She pretty much just summed it up with one word: *death*. To some, death is easier than diet. No one likes the word, so now, for better purposes, it is no longer an acceptable word that could be described by most as just a long-term change to their eating habits. It is used primarily now to get you ready for a special occasion, getting that beach or summer-vacation body. Only to get in and then get out. But, as some people experience more often than others, it is found to be just as temporary and short lived as the special event. Just like fashion can be for women. Some, if not most, dieters will tend to go back to their old eating habits, gaining it all back, if not more.

Merriam-Webster defines *diet* this way:

> a: food and drink regularly provided or consumed a
>   diet of fruits and vegetables a vegetarian diet
> b: habitual nourishment links between diet and
>   disease

c: the kind and amount of food prescribed for a person or animal for a special reason was put on a low-sodium diet

d: a regimen of eating and drinking sparingly so as to reduce one's weight going on a diet

Most will use the last in the list of the above descriptions when reflecting on the definition of diet, eating and drinking sparingly to reduce weight. They feel the anxiety instantly just thinking of dieting. Sometimes just saying the word can make you hungry. But why should it be like that? A diet is not short term; eating and getting healthy is a lifelong commitment. It is about being diligent in what you want to do and succeeding by sticking with it.

We wake up every day at the same time to get to work on time. We maintain a schedule to cut the grass and weed the garden, keeping the flowers blooming. We make sure our gas tank is full and our oil is changed. We get haircuts every six weeks. We brush our teeth at least twice a day, and we go to the dentist every six months. These are things people do without even thinking about maintaining the necessary schedules. You just do what needs to be done. Diligently. So, why is it so hard to eat in the same manner we do these other tasks? Is it a craving, a different part of the brain that is stimulated, which leads to bad food choices instead of healthy eating? I am sure food documentaries and commercials do not exactly help, because, let's face it, what you see on TV will cause cravings; you want to eat what looks good, especially when you see the fun everyone is having, all happy and laughing—that is the life for you. This is what we associate food with, while thoughts of dieting make us feel depressed. The chemical or hormone produced for that drive to eat those comfort foods you crave or just habitually eat is different than that of the satisfaction that the yard is clean or your work is completed before a deadline. But, what if you turned that satisfaction in another direction, not to satisfy you but to glorify God. Would you be willing to work toward it just has hard as the other tasks you do?

Diligence is "steady, earnest, and energetic effort: persevering application," according to Merriam-Webster. It is careful and continued hard work. It is designed for success in anything you do. It is meant to be for God, family, and work—and for taking care of yourself, including the way you eat. This is the key component of anything you want to achieve with a long-term positive effect, especially in your life, spirit, and health. Everyone has it; the ability to be diligent. Everyone is diligent in at least one thing, if not more, in his or her daily routine. The hard work is taking that same diligence and drive you use in other daily activities and applying it to your eating habits. To where this, too, is diligently achieved, and a new, better habit is formed. I know it is difficult. Most everyone's lifestyle is too busy, and fast food is too easy. So, when you're thinking about what to wear the next day and laying it out before you go to bed, why can't you take the time to think about what you are going to eat tomorrow and lay that out as well? Just like with clothes, most people who lay them out prior to going to bed rarely deviate from that choice. Chances are that you will not deviate from predetermined, packed, and ready-to-go meals. You will pick them up and take them with you, and you will eat what you already have with you and not detour to the fast-food lane. You won't be hungry to swing into a drive-thru nor, will you have the urge to overeat and oversnack, because you planned ahead. And just like when you know you need a haircut or the grass is getting too high, your body will let you know when you are hungry, and you will be ready to feed your body with the right choices you made the night before. Because you are giving your body the nutrient-dense food it needs, not the comforting, empty calories it used to crave. Easier said than done. Yes, but what if you brought God in to help you with this? Did you ever think to ask for His help?

One Sunday, the pastor of a church I visited, said you need three things to stay in line with God:

1. Prayer
2. Read the Bible and Obey
3. Intentional Relationships

Prayer is an important part of a maintained relationship with God. Every day, every moment, every chance we can we should be praying. Pray to glorify God, and pray to ask for help. God wants the glory, and He will get the glory no matter what. To be closer with Him, there are things we need to have and be diligent in every single day, in everything we do. Let's explore some of these things.

A man born in 1865 inspired many people to begin every day and every task with prayer. The youngest in his family, at the age of ten, he lost both of his parents, about eight months apart from each other, and was forced to move in with his older brother. As his family did before him, he, too, evolved to have the talent and love for music. In his lifetime, he wrote several hundred pieces of compositions, many of which were written to bring people closer to God. According to Wikipedia, *"The St. Matthew Passion* is a Passion, a sacred oratorio in 1727 for solo voices, double choir, and double orchestras. It sets chapters 26 and 27 of the Gospel of Matthew to music, with interspersed chorales and arias. It is widely regarded as one of the masterpieces of classical sacred music." On his compositions, at the top of each sheet, the letters "JJ" were found written in the corner, and at the end, the initials "SDG" were inscribed. JJ was discovered and translated to be an abbreviation for *Jesu Juva*, which means "Jesus, help me." SDG stood for *Soli Deo Gloria*, "To God alone be the glory." *Encyclopaedia Britannica* writes that, "Although he was admired by his contemporaries primarily as an outstanding harpsichordist, organist, and expert on organ building, He is now generally regarded as one of the greatest composers of all time and is celebrated as the creator of the <u>Brandenburg Concertos</u>, <u>The Well-Tempered Clavier</u>, and many more masterpieces." This great composer is no other than Johann Sebastian Bach.[81]

Bach did not do anything, not even write down one note, until he prayed for guidance, and then he finished all his work by glorifying

[81] Unknown, "J. S. Bach: Soli Deo Gloria—To the Glory of God Alone," Christianity.com, July 19, 2010, https://www.christianity.com/church/church-history/church-history-for-kids/j-s-bach-soli-deo-gloria-to-the-glory-of-god-alone-11635057.html.

God. This should be an inspiration to us all. An example of what diligence can become, and how God, if you let Him, can work through us all. You can clearly see Bach had all three needs. Prayer was there, for sure, in his music at the very beginning. Glorifying God at the end of each completed musical piece proved he had an intentional relationship with God. Some of his music was composed with the inspiration of the Bible, so this should lead us to believe he also read and obeyed.

I am not saying that this will make you a musician or composer like Bach was, but your accomplishments are endless and pure if you take God with you every step of the way. When I allow God to guide me, my progress is smoother. When I allow God to help me, my decisions are easier. So, when I eat to also glorify God, my cravings are less; I am more satisfied, and I am healing every day, physically and spiritually. I continue to make the right decisions to eat the way God intended us to eat, so I can remain healthy to serve Him, pray to Him, and glorify Him. The cravings are replaced with serenity, strength, and determination. This can replace anything you lacked within your consciousness and your desire to change the way you are now.

So now, *diet* is no longer a four-letter word you should fear. Why? If you are *Diligent in Every Thing* (D.I.E.T.), you are always DIETing and eating to glorify God.

Diligence Is Hope Maintained Every Single Day

Remember the ninety-day challenge my church did to give our tithes and offerings as God has commanded us to do? Many people, without hesitation, took that challenge and wrote to the pastor to share their experiences and the blessings they had received by doing just as they were asked to do. Some sold their houses that had been on the market for many years; others obtained raises that were years overdue, receiving more than what they asked for or were promised. I am asking you for thirty days. Give this change of eating to glorify

God, eating toward a healthier body, thirty days. Reverse the diabetes; reverse that AD that keeps you from living the normal life that you wish so much to have. What do you have to lose? Is it not worth a try to possibly have no more pills to take, no more shots, no more of whatever you wish you had less of? No more pain or worrying about where the bathroom is. Reduce your cholesterol. Reduce the pain in your joints. Give up all that processed food and fatty meals, and eat the food that God placed on this earth for us to eat. Eat the food that can heal you, and reverse that bloating, gas, and chronic exhaustion. You'll feel better, with a clearer mind, and a body that will thank you for it. Let Jesus be your portion, and your food the serving and the body to serve the Lord. Jesus gave His life for us. What are you willing to give up to glorify Him?

> And we desire that each one of you show the same diligence to the full assurance of hope until the end, that you do not become sluggish, but imitate those who through faith and patients inherit the promises.
>
> Hebrew 6:11–12 NKJV

Chapter **14**

The Plan

FIVE O'CLOCK IN THE morning comes quickly, especially when you do not even have to get up that early. With my book nearly finished, I came to what was to be the final chapter. Once again, I was at a loss as to how to tie this all together. How should I present the perfect words so that everyone who reads this book will have a good understanding of not just how to eat right and heal the body in order to be healthier and happier, but also to begin a better relationship with God? As with other chapters that had stumped me, I felt I had no clue, so I prayed.

I then got out of the bed and let the dogs out for their morning outdoor session. It was too early to feed them, but I had woken up very hungry. I fixed my breakfast and turned on the TV. I am not sure of the channel now, but I think it was Atlanta WATC, channel 57. It was an interview. Normally, I would watch Fox News, but, for some reason, I kept it on and continued to watch and listen. Dr. John Wynn was speaking about his book *Wrestling with God* and discussing his faith. Through him, God spoke to me, answering my prayer from a short while before. I could hear Him say, "Listen to this man; hear what he has to say." *Bam!* There it was, the words I will always remember: "True faith has no alternative plan." These words just brought me even closer to God. The thrill that He was working through me raised the hair on the back of my neck, and I don't even think I would have been able to speak even a word at that moment. I ran upstairs to my computer, opened the document reserved for chapter 14—now just a blank page—and typed the words I'd just heard. For the rest of that day, I just waited for more inspiration and guidance from God to complete this final chapter, which you are about to read.

Just as faith has no alternative plan, the same is true for a healthier lifestyle. Your only alternative is continuing to live unhealthfully, remaining sick, consuming several pills a day, or enduring whatever your circumstances may be in dealing with the condition(s) likely caused by poor eating habits. It took a lot of studying and trial and error to get to where I am today. But, through diligence, I found myself stronger in mind, body, and soul.

I knew eating healthier was the key, but I first had to discover what I lacked so that I could provide my body with what it needed to heal and get well. I discovered that I not only had a B_{12} deficiency, but, like most people with hypothyroidism, I also had deficiencies of selenium, iodine, magnesium, and zinc. So, to start off, I started taking supplements to ensure I was getting what I needed for my body to stop attacking my thyroid (that is, resolve the autoimmune response). These four wonders all work beautifully together to optimize thyroid function. To find out if I was iodine sufficient, I tested a few drops of Lugol's Iodine on the inside of my forearm. Within fifteen minutes, my body had absorbed all the iodine. I then began applying three to four drops daily, sometimes twice a day, until my body was absorbing three to four drops within a twenty-four-hour period. After that, I only applied the iodine as needed (once the iodine stain was gone), which became about every two days. I took two hundred milligrams of Selenium daily, along with magnesium, zinc, thytrophin PMG.

Avoid finding out the hard way, as I did, that you must not take all this at the same time. If you are on Synthroid, always take that by itself (first thing in the morning, as prescribed) at least one hour before any other medication. Do not take the selenium on an empty stomach, and do not take more than two hundred milligrams per day; it can and will make you sick. I did all of this under the guidance of my doctor, and I made sure there was no selenium in anything I was taking. You can overdose on selenium. As a result of taking it correctly and under the monitoring of my doctor, the selenium worked for me. Soon after I began taking the selenium, my doctor reduced my Synthroid dosage. When you get the thumbs up from your doctor because what you are doing works, keep doing it. For me, the key was not to take more pills, but by supplementing deficiencies, you are working toward weaning your body off prescribed medications.

This is where this book can become an awesome resource because you can learn which foods have the minerals and vitamins you need but are lacking, and where you can find those minerals and vitamins—not to mention which foods aid in healing the body. Since I was deficient in selenium, zinc, and iodine, I needed to focus on increasing my intake of whole grains. I discovered that I could get some of the required minerals just from making fresh-milled bread. Remember, your body only needs small amounts of certain minerals for optimal function, so making my own bread was a huge breakthrough, enabling me to get a certain amount of what I needed daily without increasing supplementation.

Growing up, you were told you should have three meals a day. Then, it was discovered that if you broke down those three meals into six smaller ones, you would increase your metabolism and actually lose weight. I agree that eating small amounts throughout the day is the best approach. However, it is very important to know when you are hungry and when you are full in order for this approach to work properly for your body. Eating six times a day, if not done properly, can cause you to gain weight and then become discouraged, causing you to give up quicker and begin searching for another "dieting option" (here is where yo-yo dieting got its name). Searching for a healthier lifestyle should not be expensive, difficult, or discouraging. It should be as easy as just reaching to open your refrigerator door. Everything you need is right inside there. I mean *everything*. You just have to make the effort to make sure it is stocked with the right tools, but there is one tool you won't find in that refrigerator.

Starting out, I needed help to understand how food works together when I eat. I needed to find a way to eat healthy and make sure I was eating properly and sufficiently. That meant all the food I was eating had to be nutritionally dense, allowing my body to use all the food's nutrition and not store anything unwanted. I discovered that, yes, there is an app for that: the Low-Glycal Diet, by BioFit, Inc. This app was the best tool I used to jump-start my way into not only losing weight but also optimizing my thyroid health. I wanted to eat healthier, but I also knew certain foods reacted differently in my body because of my thyroid issues. With an underactive thyroid, you tend to gain weight even when you are dieting. You can eat fruit, but if you choose the wrong fruits together, that can cause a sugar spike, and your body ends up storing excess nutrients. You are then back to either not losing weight or, worse, gaining weight. This is how I discovered that adding only half a banana to my smoothie prevented that sugar spike and most other fruits combined properly were friendly and reacted positively to my body; similarly, eating half a sandwich served me better than eating a whole one. This means one slice of bread per sandwich. You will use the app on a regular basis for a while, until you get the idea of what an actual serving is and how food can work with you or against you. It is color coded. Green indicates a good food combination; yellow means you can eat it, but be careful; and red shows that it is not a good combination—the nutrients are insufficient or will be stored, so you should only have foods that show up red, say, once a week or on special occasions. I actually found it to be fun to use this tool, seeing what combinations I could create. Since the app is on your phone, you will never leave it behind.

Back to a point raised earlier, know when you are hungry. When you get those hunger pangs (pains), your body is not hungry for food but for the nutrients contained in the food. This is why sometimes you eat till you're full, and then, an hour later, you're hungry again. It is because the food you ate lacked the nutrients that your body needs, and so your body still wants the nutrients. Without understanding this, you interpret feeling hungry simply as your body wanting more food. The solution is to change what you consume, ensuring that it is nutrient dense, which will allow your body to utilize all the nutrients. You will soon find your body craving less "junk" and more nutritious food, and you will feel hunger on a more regular basis and not suddenly after you just ate. You will be hungry less often, because the plethora of nutrients in your new choices of healthy foods will take longer for your body to utilize. Sometimes hunger is simply your body's thirst for water.

There are approximately ten different forms of false hunger. Addiction, or desire for stimulation, is one form. Tiredness experienced as a need for food is another. Thinking about, seeing, or smelling food is another. The discomfort of the body in utilizing its reserves is another. An irritation of the lining of the stomach is another. Another is the habituation to regularity, which includes habitually eating foods low in nutrient density. Avoiding a task or chore can also make you think you are hungry. Not understanding true low blood sugar can cause you to overeat as well.[82]

Robert Chuckrow states it best:

> For most people, hunger is the greatest obstacle to eating healthfully and the best way to deal with inappropriate cravings is first to experience them. Then attempt to objectively identify them. If, for example, you realize that your sensation of hunger is from an irritated stomach, that knowledge will be very helpful both in dealing with that problem and in quelling your craving. First cultivate the awareness

---

[82] Robert Chuckrow, "Understanding Hunger," "True vs. False Hunger," https://www.chuckrowtaichi.com/TrueVsFalseHunger.html.

that the hunger is false. Next, develop the tools and resolve to deal with it over the long term. Thus armed, it will be easier to dismiss any thought of eating the wrong food. Just think of how good you feel when you eat properly and are at the correct weight. Think of any health condition with which you may suffer or any excess weight you may be constantly carrying around. Analogously, if your house were always cluttered with unwanted junk, you would want to remedy this condition as soon as possible. Look at the food and ask, "Do I want that to become part of me?"[83, 84]

All that said, this is where diligence plays a huge part. You have to be aware of when you are eating and when you are actually hungry. The honor system has to kick in here. Be true to yourself, because only you know when you are actually hungry (or not) and why you are hungry.

In addition, you need to know as you are eating when to stop. Eating till you are full is never necessary to obtain optimal nutrition. Eating nutrient-dense food is the biggest key factor. Listen to your body at all times, and you will know when to stop eating. Believe it or not, most people will find that half a sandwich or a small smoothie (five to eight ounces) is enough to satisfy the body and allow it to use just those nutrients until it is ready to get some more. I promise you, your body will let you know what it needs. Timing and patience are key. After you eat, ask yourself, *Am I really still hungry?* A few hours later, you will get to eat the other half of that awesome sandwich. This is not about stuffing yourself till you are full. It is about eating till you are satisfied, till your hunger goes away. This gives your body time to digest and use what you have given it. Listen to your body, and it

---

[83]   Healthline.com, https://www.healthline.com/nutrition/why-is-fructose-bad-for-you#section1.

[84]   Robert Chuckrow, *The Intelligent Dieter's Guide* (Briarcliff Manor, NY:, Rising Mist Publications, 1997).

will tell you when it wants more. As time goes by, you will be eating healthier, getting all the nutrients your body wants and needs, when it needs them. I even have come to discover that, by the end of the day, sometimes as early as six o'clock in the evening, my body has received all the nutrients needed for the day, and I won't be hungry until the next morning. You wake up to find your bloated stomach is receding, you feel more energetic, and you know you have lost weight without even getting on the scale.

To reemphasize this is a complete lifestyle change, altering everything, perhaps even including changing your route going to work or school just to avoid the fast food drive-ins, packing food daily, and planning out everything you eat so that you won't feel hungry and need to stop for fast food. Some days you will find that you bring leftovers back home. I did, but I never left them out for the next day. I took them with me always. Every day is different, and you do not want to be away from home and not have enough food to get you back home. So, plan for everything, and prepare ahead of time when you can.

I always make enough smoothies for four days and prepare my travel pack the night before. You do not want to be caught running late and having no time to make your meals for the day. Go out and find a lunch bag that keeps things cool and will stay cool for the time you are away from home. I found one that I could put in the freezer, then, in the morning, I pull it out and fill it up with my goodies for the day. I even bought a food scale to weigh my proteins and raw cheeses, depending on my choice of protein for that day. This is not OCD; this is being diligent and having awareness and properly preparing everything you will put in your body and being in control of your portions and food choices.

Here is a sample of my daily food intake:

> An eight-ounce smoothie plus a small apple or another other single fruit; just make sure it is a true serving. This works well before you have your smoothie,

because you can save it for work; this will hold you over till you get there.

Half a sandwich that includes one slice (one ounce) of fresh-milled Bread, three to five ounces of protein (I prefer raw cheese to meat if I plan on eating meat at night or not having meat at all that day), loaded up with spinach or any raw vegetables desired (the crunchier the chew, the better), and coconut mayonnaise. Make two half sandwiches, but wrap them separately so that you are not tempted to eat both of them at the same time. (Before my milling days, If I needed to use store-bought bread. I always chose pumpernickel because it usually has less sugar than the others. I used only one slice and cut it in half.)

4. A serving of organic carrots (I would eat these sometimes with my first half sandwich if I truly felt I was still hungry.)

5. A serving of Nuts (I like pistachios, almonds, or cashews. These come in handy when heading home and stuck in traffic. These are true temptation savers for me.)

6. Plenty of water, which you need to drink throughout the day.

I know what you are thinking: *This is not enough food for the day!* Remember, you are working toward quality, not quantity, of food. You will notice, as you use the app I told you about, that your body needs fewer carbohydrates as the day draws to a close. You need most of your energy-source foods in the morning, normally before three in the afternoon. Reducing your carb intake throughout the day and increasing your protein prevents your body from storing those unused nutrients and allows it to utilize more of the proteins it needs in the evening to heal and repair at night while you sleep, forcing your body to utilize what has been stored in the past. There were plenty of times when a good small salad and a little protein, or a protein snack, was all I needed at the end of the day. Throughout the day and till the end of the day, I ate more vegetables—those great super foods—and fewer starchy foods and meats, ensuring most of my intake was in its raw state. You don't have to deprive yourself, but save meats and treats for weekends or special occasions. One small red potato is actually a serving, but if you eat it at the wrong time, it will be stored for later use because your body does not need it and will not use it beyond a certain time of the day. Awareness is key, and, again, your body will let you when it needs food and how much is necessary.

Learning to read your body and know what it needs and when it needs it will be a huge factor toward your success in this new lifestyle of eating. You will not crave those sugary foods. You will not go hungry, but you will feel healthier and more energized, you will have more clarity and focus, and soon you will be in those skinny jeans. You will notice the change in the way you feel—if not the same day, the very next day and every day thereafter. I am not one of those who has tried every diet, only to find that none worked for me. But I have tried some diets, and I never stuck with them. Mostly, I was a pill popper expecting immediate results. I was lazy; I wanted the easy way out, not having to work for the desired results. I suffered because of the decisions I made. You do have to work for it. Nothing comes easy. You have to dedicate yourself to change, and you have to make the change. No one else will do this for you. Surprisingly enough, you do not have to exercise to get good results, but what is wrong with a great walk in the morning or evening? You can use it as a way to spend time with friends or family, or you can go by yourself to mediate or just reflect with God. You have nothing to lose but a little more weight at a quicker pace, and you also give your body a great boost of endurance. If you do decide to exercise, your body will call for a little more food, so feed the need, know when to stop, and always plan ahead.

This is a lifelong commitment. Although your body will heal and you will see and reap those benefits, if you go back to eating your old way, your body will revert back. This is a lifelong commitment to continual healing and constant maintenance, and I do believe that we can change our DNA, just as it changed in those before us and passed down their diseases to us. This complex body given to us has the ability to heal on its own, given the right nutrients to provide that healing at the cellular level. I believe that with constant and consistent eating of the proper foods we were intended to eat, we can change the DNA within us and pass on those healthier cells to our unborn children, reducing the number of people suffering with the ADs discussed throughout this book. Some diseases we may have no control over; God said there would be diseases and death. But I still believe that, on an individual level, we can control and create a much healthier lifestyle for ourselves and our future children. Are you ready to change?

In conclusion, with my green tea with ginger and jasmine steaming in my favorite cup given to me by my mother, I realized that instead of running up the stairs to type this chapter and finish my book, I should have been on my knees thanking God for waking me up early and turning on the TV, for giving me all the resources needed to write His words and deliver His message. So, with that conviction festering inside me, I prayed to my Lord and Savior:

> Father, please forgive me, for I have sinned. I am not worthy of Your grace and mercy, yet You give these gifts freely and unearned. Why You have chosen me to write Your words I may never know; why You placed this task on me when there are so many others who can set out to give these words of encouragement and hope. There are others who could put these words on paper better than I, and yet You chose me. *You chose me.* I am humbled immensely by the choice You have made, yet I fear I may be a disappointment. I fear I will let down not just You but also all those reading

this book, including my family. My fears You hear, and all these concerns You already know. Thank You, God, for believing in me and giving me the strength to continue on, reminding me that the outcome and result are Yours, not mine. I am only to finish and believe in You and You only. My worries I give to You. My faith will remain true because I know You have a plan and a purpose. I know there is no alternative plan but that given by You in true faith. My faith is in You. Please give me the final words to write so that others may live and no longer be in despair; so that they will come to believe as I believe, have faith as I have faith, and have courage as I have courage. They will know that You are the only true God, the only God who truly loves each of us, the only God who gave His Son to die for us so that, although our hands may be dirty, we can raise them to praise You and be forgiven. In Christ's name, I pray. Amen.

The answer to my prayer resounded in my head with only one sentence. God says, "If I thought someone else could do it better, you wouldn't be doing it." I smiled at that, so my heart told me that maybe God was smiling and laughing too. Maybe just chuckling. In faith, there is no alternative plan; you are the one chosen to do a specific task, and in God's plan you are the only one who can do it. Well, how awesome is that?! I cannot explain the true awe I had at that very moment and complete understanding that *faith is an act*.

Still, in the back of our minds, we may think, *Really, Lord? You couldn't find anyone else?* I get how Noah was chosen to build the ark; it wasn't just that it was slim pickings back then. God knew Noah and his family were worth saving. God was not reaching down to the bottom of the barrel here when He told Noah His plans. Noah was the crème de la crème. This is just a book, not Noah's ark. Better, more-experienced authors are out there. I never wrote a book before; but, thinking like a superhero, I thought I could do it. Or could I?

Then, I thought, *How much experience did Noah have in building arks? I am pretty sure that was his first one.* It was the same for me writing my first book. Just like Noah, I was given the tools I needed to finish; neither one of us was left alone to complete the task. So, maybe I was crème de la crème too, and He wasn't reaching down to the bottom of the barrel with me either. Maybe I will be mocked and laughed at too. I don't care. Noah and I both believed and obeyed, just as others have done after him and before me. God had the same goal with Noah that He has with me and everyone else. We are all crème de la crème; He doesn't make junk. He wants us all to serve, make things better, speak out on a different perspective on life and living. There is no alternative plan. He is still in control, and He wants everyone to know that.

That said, now I come to the true conclusion, offering a way to put all this information in place for you to use to get on track with a healthier lifestyle and a better relationship with God. Know that faith heals, just as food can heal. Sit back and think about where you are today. How do you feel—not just in your body but also in your soul too? How strong is your faith in God today? Think about those obituaries we talked about. Are you a merchant of death or a missionary of charity?

Clarissa Harlowe Barton, known as Clara, is one of the most honored women in American history. Barton risked her life to bring supplies and support to soldiers in the field during the Civil War. At the age of sixty, her understanding of the ways she could provide help to people in distress guided her throughout her life. By the force of her personal example, she opened paths to the new field of volunteer service. Her intense devotion to serving others resulted in enough achievements to fill several ordinary lifetimes. For the next twenty-three years, she continued this legacy of service to humanity by establishing the American Red Cross in 1881 and serving as president of the organization until 1904.[85]

---

[85] Red Cross, About Us, http://www.redcross.org/about-us/who-we-are/history/clara-barton.

Just like Clara and others before me, God gave me a task to do. Now, I may not help as many people as Mother Teresa or Clara Barton, but I write this book in the hope that it could help at least one person. If it does, it will be just as thrilling to me as saving or helping thousands. A pastor's success is saving one soul. My success will be of the same. But my absolute success in this whole project is twofold: God gave me a job, and I obeyed; I took on the task He gave me, and I finished it. There was no alternative plan. Just as we raise our kids to know and love Christ as we do, at a certain point in their lives, we must let go and give the rest to God to handle. With this book, I must do the same. I do pray that, somewhere, someone who reads this book will change for the better. Become closer to God and use the tools in these chapters to not only have a healthy body but a healthy soul as well.

We are all given jobs to do. We all serve Christ so that we can serve others. We are here for each other, to minister, to love, and to nurture. We are the caretakers of this earth, all the great and small, the healthy and sick, the wealthy and the poor. And know that when God calls on you to do a job, you do it. It is His plan, His road that He will lead you down, and in faith there really is no alternative. You will feel so much better knowing that you did and that you did it with Him and for Him. But you have to choose to get involved in God's process. You may ask, "So, what does God want out of this?" It is simple. Maybe, hopefully, one more saved soul, one less suffering and sick person—only He knows the end result of where this will lead, but you have to start the task and finish it to find out why you were chosen and where it is going. You may be chosen to begin a task that carries on even after you're gone, like Mother Teresa, Clara Barton and the Red Cross, Martin Luther King Jr., Johann Sebastian Bach, and, someday, my mother and the Daily Bread. All of whom left, or will leave, a legacy, all fabulous examples of true servants of Christ. So, at the end of the day, you lay your head down to rest after a job well done, and for that, you will give God the glory.

So, what does God want? Just to be and only to be *Glorified*. God bless you all.

Let All Things Praise the Lord

Praise the Lord!
Praise God in His Sanctuary;
Praise Him in His mighty firmament!

Praise Him for His mighty acts;
Praise Him according to His excellent greatness!

Praise Him with the sound of the trumpet;
Praise Him with the lute and harp!
Praise Him with the timbrel and dance;
Praise Him with stringed instruments and flute

Psalm 150:1-4

SDG:

To God alone I give the glory

Recipes

Morning Smoothies

(can be doubled for two)
1/2 banana
1/2 cup blueberries
1/2 cup blackberries
1/2 cup pineapple
4 strawberries
juice of 1/2 lime (optional)
1 teaspoon coconut sugar (optional)
1 cup spinach
1/2 cup coconut water (less or more, as desired for thickness)

Combine all the ingredients in a blender. I blend all the fruit together first and then add the spinach; it seems there is more room for the spinach after the fruit is blended. To prevent a sugar spike, never use more than half a banana per serving. The coconut water helps the ease of blending all the fruit together if your blender has less power. I use a Cuisinart blender, and I need the coconut water to aid in blending and to reduce thickness. Regular water will do, but I like the benefits the coconut water adds to the smoothie.

Servings: 1

Smoothie Orange

1 medium navel orange
4 strawberries
1/2 cup blueberries
1/2 cup pineapple
1/2 banana
1/2 cup coconut water
1 cup baby spinach
1 teaspoon coconut sugar (optional)

Combine all the ingredients in a blender. I blend all the fruit together first and then add the spinach; it seems there is more room for the spinach after the fruit is blended. To prevent a sugar spike, never use more than half a banana per serving. The coconut water helps the ease of blending all the fruit together if your blender has less power. I use a Cuisinart blender, and I need the coconut water to aid in blending and to reduce thickness. Regular water will do, but I like the benefits the coconut water adds to the smoothie.

Coconut Mayonnaise

12 tablespoons extra-virgin olive oil
4 tablespoons coconut oil, melted
2 large egg yolks
1 large whole egg
3 teaspoons all-natural/organic dijon mustard
1/4 teaspoon kosher/sea salt

Mix all ingredients together, with the exception of the oils. Melt the coconut oil and mix in with the olive oil. Slowly blend the oils into the mixture. The pouring process should be very, very slow, taking five minutes or longer to pour. Add more salt sparingly, if needed, to taste.

Grilled Portabella Mushroom

(great for a meat replacement)
3–4 medium portabella caps
1 shallot, minced
4 tablespoons extra-virgin olive oil
1/4 cup balsamic vinegar

Mix the shallots, oil, and vinegar together. Placing the caps top side down, pour ingredients into mushrooms. Allow to marinate for about thirty minutes.

Place on grill, keeping the direct flames away from the mushrooms; cook on the grill for about ten minutes. Serve.

Basic Dough Recipe for Freshly Milled Flour

1 1/2 cups hot water
1/3 cup oil (I use coconut oil)
1/3 cup honey
2 teaspoons salt
1 egg (optional)
2 tablespoons lecithin (1 egg yolk for every for every tablespoon is a good substitute)
1 teaspoon gluten (optional)
4–4 1/2 cups freshly milled flour
1/2 cup flaxseed, ground in blender (optional)
1 tablespoon yeast

Combine water, oil, honey, salt, and egg. Add lecithin, gluten, and half of the flour and flaxseed. Mix thoroughly. Add yeast and enough flour to make soft dough. Knead until smooth and elastic (about five to six minutes). Let the dough rise until doubled. Shape as desired and let rise again until doubled. For two one-pound loaves, bake at 350 degrees for twenty-five to thirty minutes. If doubling the recipe, knead for eight minutes; if tripling or quadrupling, knead for twelve minutes.

Call-of-the-Fall Juicer

(perfect if you feel a cold coming on or just want something sweet like a pie)

3 sweet potatoes
2 medium carrots
1 orange, peeled
1 Granny Smith apple
1/2 inch ginger

Fill the chute of the juicer with the above ingredients. Process until all ingredients are juiced, pour into a glass, and sprinkle cinnamon on top. Enjoy!

The Skinny-on-Greens Juicer

(great for extra weight loss)

2 green apples
1 cucumber
3 cups of kale leaves

Fill the chute of the juicer with the above ingredients. Process until all ingredients are juiced and pour into a glass. Enjoy!

Three-Veggie, Three-Fruit Smoothie

3/4–1 cup water or coconut water
1 mango, pear, or apple
1 orange
1 cup blueberries, strawberries, or pineapple
3 vegetables (your choice)

Add water or coconut water to the blender. Add the fruits you chose (mango, pear, or apple; the softer fruits work best), then add an orange and the blueberries, strawberries, or pineapple (you choose; not all three).

Add the vegetables of your choice, but put them in the blender last.

Want a creamier smoothie? A quarter of an avocado will do perfectly.

Experiment with any combination to come up with your favorite.

Gluten Free Flour—If you Must

(can be used with any bread recipe)

1 cup rice flour
1 cup brown-rice flour
2/3 cup potato starch
1/3 cup tapioca starch

This will make three cups of gluten-free all-purpose flour

Need it to be self-rising? Add one one-half teaspoons of baking powder and one-half teaspoon of salt per cup of flour.

Citrus Shrimp

(easy to double recipe)

2 oranges
3 limes
2 tablespoons olive oil
3 garlic cloves
1/2 teaspoon salt, to taste
1 1/2 pounds of large shrimp, peeled

Combine all the ingredients (except the shrimp) in a blender or food processor.

Pour over the shrimp and allow to marinate for twenty minutes at room temperature.

Over medium-high heat, cook shrimp for about three minutes per side, in batches as necessary. Spoon some of the marinade in with the shrimp for extra flavor, if you like. (These are great on the grill as well.)

Provence-Style Tomatoes

4–6 large tomatoes
1 1/2 cups fresh bread crumbs
1/4 cups scallions, minced
1/4 cup basil, minced
2 tablespoons flat-leaf parsley, minced
1/2 teaspoon thyme leaves
salt and pepper (to taste)
1/2 cup of gruyère cheese
2–3 tablespoons olive oil

Preheat oven to 400 degrees.

Combine all ingredients except the cheese and oil and the salt and pepper.

Cut tomatoes (cross length), core, and remove all meat and juice.

Add salt and pepper to tomatoes.

Stuff tomatoes with combined ingredients and bake for fifteen minutes.

Thirty seconds before they are done sprinkle with cheese and drizzle with olive oil.

Serve hot or at room temperature.

Broccoli Tots

A great alternative to Tater Tots!

2 cups or 12 ounces uncooked or frozen broccoli
1 large egg
1/4 cup diced yellow onion
1/3 cup cheddar cheese
1/3 cup panko breadcrumbs
1/3 cup Italian breadcrumbs
2 tablespoons parsley
1/2 teaspoon salt
1/2 teaspoon pepper

Preheat oven to 400 degrees. Grease a baking sheet with thin layer of oil or parchment paper and set aside.

Blanch broccoli in boiling water for one minute, then remove and shock with cold tap water to stop the cooking process. Drain well.

Chop broccoli finely and mix thoroughly with egg, onions, cheddar, breadcrumbs, and seasonings. Scoop about one and one-half tablespoons of mix, using your hands or an ice-cream scoop, and gently press and form them into the shape of Tater Tots. Place on baking sheet.

Bake until golden brown and crispy (eighteen to twenty-four minutes. Turn them halfway through the baking process. Remove from the oven and enjoy.

Sweet-and-Spicy Citrus-Infused Water

8 cups water
1 tangerine, sliced thin
1 lemon, sliced thin
1 pear, sliced thin
1 red Thai chili pepper, sliced thin
4–5 sprigs cilantro

Combine all ingredients and refrigerate for twelve hours to infuse all the flavors.

Four-Carrot Gold (Get Your Beta-Carotene On)

4 carrots
2 large kale leaves, stems removed
1 Golden Delicious apple
fresh ginger, to taste

Fill the chute of the juicer with the above ingredients. Process until all ingredients are juiced. Serve over ice.

Orange You Glad You Juiced Today

1 orange
5 carrots

2 to 3 handfuls spinach
1/2 inch ginger
cinnamon, to taste

Fill the chute of the juicer with the above ingredients. Process until all ingredients are juiced. Serve over ice.

Cha-Cha-Cha Chia

1 orange, peeled
1/2 banana, peeled
5 whole strawberries
4 peach slices
1/2 cup açai berries
2 tablespoons chia seeds

Mix all ingredients in a blender. Pour into a glass and enjoy.

Roast Chicken with Lemon and Rosemary Roast Potatoes

41/2-pound free-range, organic chicken
4 pounds potatoes (I prefer red potatoes)
1 small lemon
1 whole bulb garlic, broken into cloves
1 handful fresh thyme
1 handful fresh rosemary leaves, picked off
salt and pepper (to rub into raw chicken)

Wash the chicken under cold running water and dry thoroughly with paper towels.

Rub the chicken inside and out with a generous amount of salt and ground pepper. If you are able to, do this several hours before; cover and refrigerate.

Preheat oven to 375 degrees.

Bring a large pan of salted water to a boil. Cut potatoes into small pieces (about the size of golf balls), put them into the water with whole lemon and garlic cloves (do not throw these out), and cook for six minutes.

Drain potatoes and allow them to steam in the covered pan for one minute; remove lemon and garlic. Toss potatoes (while still hot) into roasting pan you will use to roast the chicken.

While the lemon is still hot, carefully pierce it, eight to ten times.

Remove chicken from the refrigerator, pat dry with a paper towel, and rub olive oil all over chicken.

Insert the whole lemon, garlic cloves, and thyme into the cavity of the chicken. Place chicken into roasting pan with potatoes, and place pan into preheated oven for forty-five minutes, making sure to baste it every twenty minutes or so.

Remove roasting pan from oven. Move chicken to a plate. Some of the juices from the chicken will be left behind, so toss potatoes into juices from chicken; add rosemary leaves and spread potatoes to leave space for the chicken to be placed. Put chicken back into roasting pan and cook for an additional forty-five minutes, or until chicken is fully cooked and potatoes are a golden brown.

Remove garlic and lemon. For added flavor, you can mash the garlic out of the skin, squeeze the juice from the lemon, mix them together, and rub mixture all over the chicken. Discard sprigs of thyme.

Butternut Bisque

3 tablespoons butter
1 medium onion
2 garlic cloves, sliced
1/2 teaspoon dried thyme

1/4 teaspoon ground cinnamon
1/4 teaspoon cayenne pepper (optional)
coarse salt (to taste)
1 large butternut squash, peeled, seeded, and cut into 1-inch cubes
1 can (14 1/2 ounces) low-sodium chicken broth
1 cup half-and-half
5 cups water
1 tablespoon fresh lemon juice

In a large saucepan, heat butter over medium heat. Add onion, garlic, thyme, cinnamon, and cayenne, making sure to stir occasionally. Cook for five to seven minutes, or until onions are soft.

Add squash, broth, half-and-half, and water. Bring to a boil, reduce heat to simmer, and cook for another twenty minutes.

Place in a blender until smooth (you may need to do this in batches). Stir in lemon juice.

Garnish with sour cream and/or cayenne, if desired.

Iced Green Tea with a Citrus Punch

5 cups water
1/4 cup lime juice
3 limes, sliced
1/4 cup lemon juice
5 tea bags of green tea (jasmine works well)
1/4 cup honey
18 mint leaves

Bring two cups of water to a boil in a medium saucepan; add tea bags.

Allow tea to steep for about three minutes.

With a large spoon, carefully squeeze tea bags to extract the tea further, and then discard tea bags.

Add and stir in honey until dissolved.

Pour lemon juice and lime juice into a large pitcher. Add tea mixture.

Add three cups of cold water. Stir until blended well.

More honey can be added, if desired.

Serve over ice and garnish each glass with a lemon slice and mint leaves.

Need help? Want more recipes? Contact me or visit my website: www.tamerashearon.com.
https://www.facebook.com/eatingtoglorifygod/

About the Author

TAMERA SHEARON, A MOTHER (of three girls) and a grandmother, considers her family her greatest accomplishment. Born in California, she moved to Georgia with her family at a very young age and still resides in Atlanta to this day. A Desert Storm veteran and a retired firefighter, she has found that being a part-time real-estate agent helps her serve her community in another way.

This is her first published book, and she hopes to have many more to follow, reaching out to others looking for Christ in faith and in healing. By sharing her experiences and what she has learned, she hopes to help others find answers that they have been looking for.

When Tamera is not writing, managing, or selling real estate, she finds every opportunity to spend time with her family and friends. Her favorite place to be is anywhere that has a beach, but the place where she most loves to go is beautiful Charleston, South Carolina.

You can contact her with questions or comments through her website, www.tamerashearon.com, or via email at tamera@tamerashearon.com. More information about her can be found on her website, where you can also sign up for newsletters, blog posts, and notifications on the next book release.

CPSIA information can be obtained
at www.ICGtesting.com
Printed in the USA
LVHW022003140821
695337LV00003B/361